RAND | SOCIAL AND ECONOMIC WELL-BEING

T0302900

Evaluation of North Carolina's Pathways from Prison to Postsecondary Education Program

Lois M. Davis, Michelle A. Tolbert

Prepared for the Laughing Gull Foundation and the Vera Institute of Justice

For more information on this publication, visit www.rand.org/t/RR2957

Library of Congress Cataloging-in-Publication Data is available for this publication.
ISBN: 978-1-9774-0262-2

Published by the RAND Corporation, Santa Monica, Calif.
© Copyright 2019 RAND Corporation
RAND® is a registered trademark.

Support RAND
Make a tax-deductible charitable contribution at
www.rand.org/giving/contribute

www.rand.org

Preface

The Vera Institute of Justice's Pathways from Prison to Postsecondary Education Project was a five-year, multistate demonstration project funded by the Ford Foundation, the Sunshine Lady Foundation, the Open Society Foundations, the Bill and Melinda Gates Foundation, and the W. K. Kellogg Foundation. In 2013, Pathways funded pilot projects in three states—Michigan, New Jersey, and North Carolina—through a competitive selection process. Pathways encouraged participating states to create a continuum of education and reentry support services that begin in prison and continue in the community after release until students achieve a degree or professional certification. Each state was provided incentive funding for a four-year pilot, with the fifth year to be used to analyze the impact and outcomes of this demonstration project. In addition, the Laughing Gull Foundation and Vera Institute of Justice provided funding to evaluate the community component of North Carolina's Pathways Program in order to (1) document students' experiences as they returned to local communities to continue their education and (2) identify the factors that facilitated or hindered their ability to remain in the Pathways Program and earn a degree or credential. The RAND Corporation, in partnership with RTI International, was chosen to evaluate the Pathways demonstration project. This report focuses specifically on the evaluation of the North Carolina Pathways Program.

These findings should be of interest to state departments of corrections and public safety, community colleges and universities, corrections officials, educators, and policymakers who are interested in implementing postsecondary education programs and, specifically, college programs for incarcerated adults.

Justice Policy Program

RAND Social and Economic Well-Being is a division of the RAND Corporation that seeks to actively improve the health and social and economic well-being of populations and communities throughout the world. This research was conducted in the Justice Policy Program within RAND Social and Economic Well-Being. The program focuses on such topics as access to justice, policing, corrections, drug policy, and court system reform, as well as other policy concerns pertaining to public safety and criminal and civil justice. For more information, email justicepolicy@rand.org.

Contents

Figures and Tables

Figures

Tables

Summary

In 2013, the Ford Foundation, the Sunshine Lady Foundation, the Open Society Foundations, the Bill and Melinda Gates Foundation, and the W. K. Kellogg Foundation funded a five-year, multistate demonstration project, Pathways from Prison to Postsecondary Education, which was led by the Vera Institute of Justice. Through a competitive selection process, Pathways funded pilot projects in three states—Michigan, New Jersey, and North Carolina. Each state was given incentive funding of up to $2 million in order to offer educational programming and reentry support services for incarcerated adults, with a planned evaluation to be conducted after sufficient outcome data could be collected to analyze the impact and outcomes of the demonstration project.

Pathways encouraged participating states to create a continuum of education and reentry support services that begin in prison and continue in the community after release until students achieve a degree or professional certification. The demonstration project had the following overarching goals:

- increase postsecondary education (PSE) attainment among incarcerated and recently released individuals
- increase employability and earnings and break the cycle of intergenerational poverty
- reduce recidivism and improve quality of life in neighborhoods disproportionately impacted by crime and incarceration
- demonstrate that access to PSE and support services for people currently and formerly incarcerated can be done cost-effectively.

To help incarcerated individuals obtain a PSE degree or credential, the pilot states provided participants with PSE during at least the two years prior to their release from prison. Pilot states also provided participants with support and assistance for entering college and completing their PSE through the two years following their release. In order to increase educational persistence and completion rates among participants, the pilot states also provided extensive case planning in prison and in the community, remedial educational programming, college-readiness classes, and college counseling.

The educational programs were provided in partnership with local colleges (both community colleges and universities).

Through a competitive selection process, Vera chose the RAND Corporation, in partnership with RTI International, to evaluate the Pathways demonstration project. There were two phases to the evaluation. The first phase was a process evaluation that focused on the implementation of the in-prison component of the three pilot Pathways Programs in Michigan, New Jersey, and North Carolina. The second phase of the evaluation focused on the community component. The Laughing Gull Foundation and Vera provided funding to RAND and RTI International to conduct a process evaluation of the community component of North Carolina's Pathways Program in order to (1) document students' experiences as they returned to local communities to continue their education and (2) identify the factors that facilitated or hindered their ability to remain in the Pathways Program and earn a degree or credential. This second-phase process evaluation focused specifically on North Carolina's Pathways Program (Vera Institute of Justice, 2012a). This report presents the findings of our evaluation of the in-prison and community components of the North Carolina Pathways Program.

We used a multimethod approach to evaluate the in-prison and community components of the North Carolina Pathways Program. With respect to the in-prison component, we conducted two rounds of site visits to North Carolina in spring and summer 2014. Using a semistructured interview protocol, we conducted 25 in-person interviews with a range of stakeholders involved in planning for and implementing the program. At the correctional-facility level, these stakeholders included superintendents and assistant superintendents, correctional supervisors, education staff, college instructors, and the Pathways team; at the headquarters level, stakeholders included state corrections officials and the North Carolina Department of Public Safety (NCDPS) Pathways administrator. In addition, using a semistructured discussion guide, we conducted focus-group discussions with 13 Pathways students during October 2014.

To evaluate the community component, we conducted several rounds of site visits for each of the three release communities in North Carolina—Asheville, Charlotte, and Greenville—in 2016 and 2017. We used semistructured discussion guides to facilitate the interviews and focus-group discussions with 38 Pathways students. We also conducted 37 in-depth interviews with Pathways Program staff, reentry staff, community college staff, housing providers, and probation and parole officers (PPOs) involved in the Pathways Program. These interviews also included state-level discussions with NCDPS staff responsible for designing, implementing, and overseeing the Pathways Program.

North Carolina's Pathways Program

Prior to Pathways, incarcerated individuals in North Carolina could enroll in college correspondence courses, but there was no coordinated effort to provide a path toward a postsecondary degree or credential. Furthermore, there was no coordination around reentry into society. The Pathways Program was designed to address these limitations and to expand and strengthen the PSE and reentry services available to individuals incarcerated in North Carolina's correctional system.

The Pathways Program was led by the NCDPS Office of Reentry Programs and Services in collaboration with the NCDPS Community Corrections and the North Carolina Community College System (NCCCS). NCDPS used a variety of inputs (or resources) to implement its Pathways initiative, including its existing infrastructure and partnerships with NCCCS and local reentry councils (LRCs). North Carolina received $1 million in incentive funding to implement Pathways and was required to provide an overall match of at least 25 percent, with 15 percent in the form of a cash match (from public or private sources) and 10 percent in-kind to be distributed over the four years of the demonstration project. In-kind resources included assistance from state-level staff at NCDPS and NCCCS and staff in the participating correctional facilities and release communities (e.g., community college staff and LRCs).

While incarcerated, Pathways students had the option of earning a certificate (12–18 semester credit courses), a diploma in general education, or an Associate of Applied Science (AAS) degree. College courses were taught in person by local community college professors in six correctional facilities. Additional in-prison supports included remedial instruction in English and math, tutoring, study hall or study groups, dedicated case managers, and computer training and internet access. Prerelease supports included development of a transition plan, referral to services, and assistance with applying for financial aid and completing college applications.

Upon release, North Carolina Pathways students were expected to continue their educational coursework or to gain full-time employment and were provided with reentry and other services needed to support their educational persistence and attainment. Participants in the Pathways pilot returned to one of three release communities—Charlotte, Asheville, or Greenville—which were selected because of the presence of local community colleges and reentry infrastructure. The LRCs provided a range of reentry services to students and received funding to hire a Pathways navigator to serve as a liaison between the students and the local community colleges. Postrelease activities included college courses; financial support for college tuition and assistance in applying for federal student aid; and assistance with housing, childcare, transportation, and employment. NCDPS also asked its Community Corrections district supervisors to assign the students PPOs who would be supportive of the Pathways Program.

Through Pathways, NCDPS hoped that participants would achieve the following core outcomes: college enrollment, persistence, and completion; attainment of certificates, diplomas, and degrees; gainful employment, either part-time or full-time, and increased earnings; and reductions in recidivism, including fewer community supervision violations and instances of misconduct.

Results

We provide a brief summary of the key findings from the evaluation. In addition, we identified several lessons learned from the evaluation, which we summarize here, but which are discussed in more detail in the main report.

Pathways students were seen as dedicated to furthering their education. For the most part, Pathways students were seen by program staff, instructors, and reentry staff as committed to furthering their education. The Pathways students we interviewed were grateful for the opportunity to participate in the program, with many seeing it as an important chance to further their education and turn their lives around.

It takes time to set up these types of programs. An overarching lesson learned was that it takes a long time to implement a prison-based and community-based college program with multiple partners for a population with diverse education and reentry needs. In general, the staff and students reported feeling that a longer commitment (a minimum of five years) was needed for this type of initiative.

It takes more time for students to earn credentials and complete college coursework while incarcerated than it would if they were out in the community. The amount of developmental coursework Pathways students needed initially was more extensive than originally anticipated, which truncated the time allotted for college coursework in prison. The staff supporting the Pathways Program reported wishing that they could have offered students more time to enable them to earn a credential prior to release. Similarly, some of the Pathways students were released near the end of the program and, therefore, received less reentry support than their peers did.

The student selection process could have been improved to ensure that those selected were committed and motivated to furthering their education and to ensure that the Pathways Program was aligned with their career interests. Despite North Carolina's extensive screening processes, not all selected students assimilated well into the program in the first year, and a few left the program for personal reasons or misconduct. Student recruitment and selection are resource-intensive and time-intensive processes and adjustments had to be made (e.g., North Carolina relaxed its selection criteria to yield a sufficient pool of individuals eligible to apply to the program).

The program needs to allow students to change educational paths upon release. Because of a state law, postsecondary programs in North Carolina state prisons were limited to a terminal AAS degree. The AAS programs offered in prison were for only three majors (business administration, computer information technology [IT], and entrepreneurship), which did not always align with students' career interests. Several students changed their majors once they were out in the community.

Funding was inconsistent across release communities. The amount of time the different cohorts were in the in-prison component of the Pathways Program varied from two years to less than one year, which meant that some students received only one year of support while incarcerated and even less support once released. In addition, although each release community received the same budget from the Pathways initiative, the funding was spent differently depending on the size and needs of the student population and available community resources. Variation in how the funding was spent caused trust and communication problems and created uncertainty among the reentry staff about the resources they had to work with. Furthermore, the reentry staff was on the front line in communicating these changes to Pathways students, who were bewildered and who mistrusted what was being told to them.

Having only three release communities made sense in terms of resources but meant that students had to trade off continuing their education or moving to be near family. There were several advantages to having only three release communities, both from a resource perspective and because it enabled NCDPS to build up a robust reentry infrastructure in those communities and work with community colleges committed to the Pathways Program. However, it also meant that some students had to choose between continuing their education and moving to be near their families. This was a key factor cited in students' decisions to leave the Pathways Program upon release.

Reentry supports were critical for students to be able to stay in educational programs. Reentry was a very challenging time for Pathways students. Within a few weeks of being released, the students were expected to enroll in college full-time; secure part-time employment; find suitable housing arrangements; address transportation needs; reunite with family members; and, in some cases, resume parental and financial responsibilities for their families while managing and seeking treatment for any substance abuse, depression, anxiety, or other mental health issues. Housing, employment, and transportation were among the top referrals to services provided to Pathways students, followed by family services and substance abuse treatment services.

Family played a key role in students' decisions and success. Family can play a positive supporting role or represent a stressor because of the pressures it may place on students; specifically, family can encourage students to continue their education or pressure them to find full-time employment and help support the family.

Having a Pathways navigator and trusted persons of authority was important. Most interviewees reported feeling that the Pathways navigator role was essential and was an important source of support for many of the students. Having a navigator or a trusted person of authority who could help link students to reentry services and help them navigate applying for college and financial aid and signing up and beginning to take classes clearly was critical to students' success. This study also showed the importance of recruiting and training PPOs who are supportive of education and understand the program to work with the Pathways students.

Having the Pathways Program embedded in NCDPS was an asset. Having Department of Corrections senior leadership support and a senior administrator who was effective within that organization (as was the case here) was key to solving problems, getting and maintaining support at all levels of the department, and understanding the concerns of both correctional and educational staff and how to address such concerns.

There is a need for staff training and support. A key lesson learned was that those involved in making Pathways work need clear expectations and defined responsibilities. For many college instructors, teaching in a correctional environment was a new experience, and some found the requirements and procedures to be onerous or confusing. It also was important to reach out to and educate correctional facilities staff (including superintendents, assistant superintendents, correctional officers, and facility-based education staff) on an ongoing basis to get them on board and continually reinforce the program's goals and structure.

Good communication takes time and is critical to the success of the program. At various points, there were misunderstandings about what was promised to the students, the expectations of the program, how the Pathways students would fit into the larger correctional environment, and other areas of concern.

The Pathways Program required commitment and sacrifices from all of the stakeholders involved. Students had to agree to be moved to the prison facilities where the program was being implemented and to be released to one of three communities that may be far away from their families. Students also had to agree to remain in medium-custody facilities to complete the in-prison component of the program. Facilities had to commit staff time to coordinate the program with other in-prison programming, agree to allow students to live in separate housing units, and provide additional studying space. LRC staff had to dedicate the majority of their staff time to the Pathways students and develop or strengthen relationships with community colleges, transitional housing managers, and other community service providers. State administrations had to provide 25-percent match funding and staff time to plan, implement, and manage the program; agree to such policy changes as inmate transfers to Pathways-designated facilities; and place education holds to ensure that students stayed in designated facilities until they completed the program.

Recommendations for Other States on Implementing a Pathways-Like Model

Based on the findings and lessons learned, we make the following recommendations:

- Structure the in-prison component of the college program to allow enough time for students to build general credit and earn certifications prior to release.
- Consider eliminating the state restriction on the types of postsecondary degree programs that can be offered in prison.
- Provide specific training to those staff members (e.g., custody, agency, reentry, and PPO staff) who will work with the students on an ongoing basis so that they understand the context and parameters of the program and can better support participants.
- Structure the program to allow students to initially attend college part-time in the community upon their release from prison. This would allow them to get acclimated and go through the reentry adjustment process and would relieve the stress of trying to go to college full-time while working full-time.
- Include enough release communities in the program so that students can live near their families and other supports.
- Invest in reentry infrastructure to ensure that robust reentry supports are available to students.
- Ensure that community colleges and other education providers are part of the reentry planning and other processes to facilitate students' enrollment and reenrollment postrelease.
- Ensure that a navigator and other trusted persons of authority are in place. The Pathways navigator role was an essential source of support for many students and should be a full-time position. It is important that parole officers understand these programs and support individuals' participation in them.
- Have a dedicated, full-time program administrator for at least the first few years of program implementation. This individual would need to facilitate and build partnerships to support the in-prison and community components of the program. This individual also would need to be effective in addressing policy barriers.
- Ensure that long-term funding options are in place to sustain a college program, such as the Pathways Program, once initial grant or foundation funding has ended.

How Pathways Has Affected Prison Programming in North Carolina

NCDPS continues to find ways to fund different components of Pathways after the demonstration project ended. Pathways has had an impact on how NCDPS approaches higher education in prison and reentry planning. Pathways laid the groundwork for and showed what reentry planning should look like. It also has led to more coordination among prisons and PPOs and community resources. Importantly, because of Pathways, education has now become the fourth pillar of the department's reentry focus, which includes housing, employment, and transportation as the other three pillars. In addition, NCDPS has set up a PSE advisory committee as a result of Pathways that continues to discuss what prison education in North Carolina should entail. Pathways also has underscored the importance of technology in education, with the department's IT staff having developed their own intranet platform (called i-Net) to support PSE in prison and to provide limited internet access for these programs.

Acknowledgments

We wish to express our appreciation to the North Carolina Department of Public Safety and the Pathways Program. In particular, we appreciate the input, guidance, and support we received from the Director of Reentry Programs and Services, Nicole Sullivan, and reentry managers Allison Jourdan and Doug Pardue. We also appreciate the assistance and input provided by the local reentry councils in the three release communities—most notably, Lindsley Doddridge and Brent Bailey of the Buncombe County Reentry Council in Asheville; Hope Marshall of Mecklenburg Re-Entry Services in Charlotte; and Joyce Jones, formerly of Life of NC/Strive NC in Greenville, who facilitated our access to the Pathways students and provided input on the program. We are also grateful for the time and feedback from numerous local reentry council staff, community college staff, probation and parole officers, transitional housing managers, and other community stakeholders in the three release communities who participated in interviews.

We are especially grateful for the Pathways students' time and input. They participated in focus groups and interviews while incarcerated and after release from prison to help us understand their goals and experiences with the Pathways Program; the education, instructional supports, and reentry services available to them; and the factors that facilitated or hindered their persistence with and completion of the program. They also provided thoughtful feedback on how the program might be improved.

We are also thankful for the funding support provided by the Laughing Gull Foundation and the Vera Institute of Justice. This work has benefited greatly from the guidance we received from Meg (Coward) Baesmith, Hez Norton, and Toya Wall (formerly) of the Laughing Gull Foundation and from Fred Patrick, Margaret diZerega, and Ruth Delaney of the Vera Institute of Justice.

Finally, we would like to thank our RAND Corporation colleague Robert Bozick for the support he provided in developing the logic model and in assessing the in-prison component of the Pathways Program in North Carolina. We also appreciate the thoughtful insights provided by our technical reviewers, including Matthew Mizel of RAND, Susan Turner of the University of California-Irvine, and Susan Lockwood Roberts of Nexus Point Consulting, LLC.

Abbreviations

AAS	Associate of Applied Science
AB-Tech	Asheville-Buncombe Technical Community College
CPCC	Central Piedmont Community College
CTE	career technical education
DAC	Division of Adult Correction
DOC	Department of Corrections
DoE	U.S. Department of Education
FAFSA	Free Application for Federal Student Aid
FTE	full-time equivalent
GED	general equivalency diploma
GPA	grade point average
IHEP	Institute for Higher Education Policy
IRB	institutional review board
IT	information technology
LRC	local reentry council
NCCCS	North Carolina Community College System
NCDPS	North Carolina Department of Public Safety
NJ-STEP	New Jersey Scholarship and Transformative Education in Prisons

PEP   Prison Education Program

PPO   probation and parole officer

PSE   postsecondary education

TABE   Test of Adult Basic Education

TAN   Transitional Aftercare Network

WRAT   Wide Range Achievement Test

CHAPTER ONE

Introduction

In this chapter, we provide some background on the Vera Institute of Justice's Pathways from Prison to Postsecondary Education Project (Pathways). That background consists of a discussion of higher education in U.S. prisons, the policy context in which the Pathways Program exists, and a discussion of the Pathways Program in general with a focus on North Carolina as the basis for our current project. We then explain this project and the approach we took.

Higher Education in U.S. Prisons

A meta-analysis by Davis et al. (2013) provides the most recent evidence on the effectiveness of correctional education and how it is being provided today. The RAND Corporation was awarded a grant under the Second Chance Act to conduct a national assessment of the effectiveness of correctional education in the United States. To do so, RAND researchers undertook a comprehensive literature review of both published and unpublished studies between 1980 and 2011 and synthesized the findings using a meta-analysis in order to assess what is known about the effectiveness of correctional education programs in helping to reduce recidivism and improve postrelease employment outcomes for incarcerated adults in state prisons. Davis et al. (2013) estimated that participation in correctional education programs (whether general equivalency diploma [GED] preparation, vocational training, or postsecondary education [PSE] programs) reduced an individual's risk of recidivism overall by 13 percentage points. The reduction was even greater for incarcerated individuals who participated in PSE programs. Davis et al. (2013) estimated that participation in college or PSE programs reduced an individual's risk of recidivating by 16 percentage points compared with those who did not participate in correctional education programs. This translates to a 49-percent reduction in the odds ratio for PSE, indicating that individuals who participate in higher education programs while incarcerated are roughly half as likely to recidivate as those who do not participate in any type of correctional education program. An update of the meta-analysis to include more-recent studies (through 2017) found that these results still hold (Bozick et al., 2018). Davis et al.'s (2013) analysis also showed that these programs are cost-effective. It estimated that for every dollar spent on correctional education programs, taxpayers save $4 to $5 on three-year reincarceration costs.[1]

Despite these findings, incarcerated individuals had relatively low participation rates in PSE programs—rates that varied from state to state. A 2011 report on post-secondary correctional education policy by the Institute for Higher Education Policy (IHEP) found that from 2009 to 2010, only 6 percent of individuals incarcerated in U.S. prison systems reported being enrolled in PSE programs (Gorgol and Sponsler, 2011).[2] Moreover, the rate of completion of college degrees was quite low. States reported that approximately 9,900 incarcerated persons earned a certificate in the 2009–2010 academic year, 2,200 associate's degrees were awarded, and nearly 400 students earned bachelor's degrees. These results represented a modest increase over findings from the previous 2005 IHEP report (Erisman and Contardo, 2005). The reasons for differences in completion rates include that certificate programs take much less time to complete than most degree programs do, most incarcerated individuals can attend college courses only part-time, and individuals face several obstacles in accumulating enough credits to earn a degree while incarcerated. Such obstacles include frequent transfers between correctional facilities, resulting in an individual being moved to a facility that does not offer college courses; being released from prison prior to completing a degree or certificate program; or dropping out of a higher education program that interferes with the individual's prison work assignment(s). Community colleges provided the majority of postsecondary correctional education programs (68 percent), followed by public four-year institutions (16 percent) and private, nonprofit, four-year institutions (10 percent; Erisman and Contardo, 2005). The remaining 6 percent of programs were provided by other educational institutions (specifically, less than two-year public; two-year and less than two-year private nonprofit; and four-year, two-year, and less than two-year private for-profit colleges).

A more recent survey of all 50 state correctional education directors by Davis et al. (2014) found that only 32 states reported offering some type of PSE, and that states with medium or large prison populations were more likely to offer such courses than smaller states. PSE in 28 states was paid for by incarcerated individuals and their families or by private funding through foundations or individual donations (20 states); state funding was used in 16 states.[3] Only 12 states reported using college or university

---

[1] This is a conservative estimate because Davis et al. (2013) took only the direct costs of education programs and incarceration into account. Indirect costs, such as costs to the victims and the criminal justice system, were not included in the estimate.

[2] This report surveyed correctional education administrators in all 50 states and the Federal Bureau of Prisons and received responses from 43 states and the Bureau.

[3] The categories of funding are not mutually exclusive. PSE programs could be paid for by a variety of funders.

funding to cover the costs of PSE, and only a few states used inmate benefits or welfare funds.

Policy Context

The Pathways Program came at a time when interest in providing college programs to incarcerated adults in the United States had been growing. In the past five years, there has been a resurgence of interest at the federal and state levels in expanding higher education in prison, and particularly in expansions that offer a path to degrees or industry-recognized credentials. For example, in 2015, the U.S. Department of Education (DoE) implemented a three-year experimental program called the Second Chance Pell Experimental Sites Initiative that temporarily lifted the federal ban on Pell Grants to incarcerated individuals who otherwise met Title IV eligibility requirements.[4] Pell Grants could be used to help pay for incarcerated individuals' PSE and training, as long as an individual was eligible to be released from prison.[5] Sixty-seven colleges and universities in 27 states were selected to participate in the initiative, authorizing them to enroll up to 12,000 incarcerated students to receive Pell Grants (Wexler, 2016). Many educators, policymakers, and researchers viewed the Second Chance Pell Experimental Sites Initiative as an important opportunity to expand access to PSE programs and to test the feasibility of making Pell Grants available to those who would otherwise meet the Title IV eligibility requirements.

In addition, a number of states (e.g., New York, California, and New Jersey) have expanded PSE programs in their prisons. Whether as the result of a state or federal initiative, PSE opportunities can range from career technical education (CTE) programs and apprenticeships that lead to industry-recognized credentials to credit-bearing programs that lead to postsecondary degrees (e.g., associate and bachelor's degrees or higher) (Davis et al., 2014; Erisman and Contardo, 2005).

In 2018, the Formerly Incarcerated Reenter Society Transformed Safely Transitioning Every Person Act, known as the FIRST STEP Act, which places increased emphasis on providing education programs in federal prisons, passed the U.S. House of Representatives (U.S. House of Representatives, 2018). Among its provisions, the FIRST STEP Act would allow inmates to obtain "earned time credits" by participating in more vocational and rehabilitative programs, including education programs. Mem-

---

[4] Prior to the 1994 Crime Bill that President Bill Clinton signed into law, those who had been incarcerated in prison were eligible to receive Pell Grants to help cover the costs of participating in college programs. Pell Grants were a key source of funding of PSE for incarcerated individuals. However, in 1994, Congress amended the Higher Education Act to eliminate Pell Grant eligibility for students incarcerated in federal and state prisons (Crayton and Neusteter, 2008).

[5] Individuals with a death sentence or a life without parole sentence were not eligible to participate in the Second Chance Pell Experimental Sites Initiative.

bers of Congress also are considering legislation to reinstate incarcerated individuals' access to Pell Grants. In February 2018, Senator Brian Schatz of Hawaii introduced the Restoring Education and Learning (REAL) Act, which would restore Pell Grant eligibility to incarcerated people (U.S. Senate, 2018; Kreighbaum, 2018).

There are different perspectives about whether PSE programs in prison should lead to academic degrees or industry-recognized credentials. In general, many educators and criminal justice experts think that PSE programs in prison should result in some type of credential (e.g., an education certificate or postsecondary education degree) that is recognized by employers, colleges, and universities. Such experts also argue that the credentials earned should be "stackable" and that the program and class credits earned be transferrable to other postsecondary institutions so that the coursework completed in prison can contribute to furthering individuals' education and advancing their careers postrelease (Davis et al., 2014; Erisman and Contardo, 2005).

Given these changes in the field, the Pathways Program was seen as an important program model for providing PSE, with the potential to inform the debate about the types of credentials that should be offered in prison. The Pathways Program addressed the following key questions:

- How should in-prison college programs be structured to enable incarcerated students to earn credentials and, ultimately, college degrees?
- Who are the key stakeholders and what are their roles in supporting these types of programs?
- What other types of supports do incarcerated students need to be successful in their college program?
- What prerelease planning and supports are needed to facilitate the transition of a student to the community and the continuation of their education out in the community?
- What reentry and educational services and supports do students need out in the community to facilitate completion of their education programs?
- What factors either facilitated or hindered the implementation of these programs and what adjustments were made to address them?
- What are the key lessons learned and outcomes?

With that policy context and a sense of how the Pathways Program fit into it, we now turn to a brief overview of the program itself.

The Pathways Program

The Vera Institute of Justice's Pathways from Prison to Postsecondary Education Project was a five-year, multistate demonstration project funded by the Ford Foundation, the Sunshine Lady Foundation, the Open Society Foundations, the Bill and Melinda Gates Foundation, and the W. K. Kellogg Foundation. The Vera Institute of Justice developed a model grounded in research that demonstrated (1) the lack of education common to correctional populations and (2) the role that increased educational attainment plays in keeping formerly incarcerated people out of prison and in helping them become contributing members of families and communities (Vera Institute of Justice, 2012b; Vera Institute of Justice, 2014). See Appendix A for a detailed overview of the demonstration project.

In 2013, Pathways funded pilot projects in three states—Michigan, New Jersey, and North Carolina—through a competitive selection process. Pathways encouraged participating states to create a continuum of education and reentry support services that begins in prison and continues in the community after release until the student has achieved a degree or professional certification.

The Pathways demonstration project in each of the three selected states had the following overarching goals:

- increase PSE attainment among incarcerated and recently released individuals
- increase employability and earnings and break the cycle of intergenerational poverty
- reduce recidivism and improve quality of life in neighborhoods disproportionately affected by crime and incarceration
- demonstrate that access to PSE and support services for people currently and formerly incarcerated can be cost-effective.

To help incarcerated individuals obtain a PSE degree or credential, the three pilot states provided participants with PSE during at least the two years prior to their release from prison and provided support and assistance with entering college and completing their PSE through the two years following their release.[6] To increase educational persistence and completion rates among participants, the three pilot states also provided extensive case planning both in prison and out in the community, remedial educational programming, college-readiness classes, and college counseling. The educational programs were provided in partnership with local colleges (both community colleges and universities).

Pilot states received up to $2 million in incentive funding to offer educational programming and reentry support services to incarcerated adults. The incentive funding was designed to repurpose and leverage existing revenue streams and encourage new public and private funds in support of the proposed efforts. In order to qualify for the funding, the three states had to submit detailed descriptions of their program

---

[6]   New Jersey did not follow the two years prior to release rule; rather, a student would be able to complete one semester of college coursework to participate in its Pathways Program, known as the New Jersey Scholarship and Transformative Education in Prisons (NJ-STEP) program.

models and plans for achieving their objectives. States also had to comply with the following two core requirements (Vera Institute of Justice, 2012b):

- Provide an overall match of at least 25 percent, with 15 percent in the form of a cash match (from public and/or private sources) and 10 percent in-kind contributions to be distributed over the four years of the demonstration project.
- Convene a leadership team of public and private stakeholders to oversee the development of the work and financing plans and sign the application affirming that they support the plans as presented. Members of the leadership team also had to be willing to continue to provide oversight of the implementation, hold agencies and leaders to their commitments, and support the project's continuation and expansion if the pilots were successful.

In addition, pilot states were required to have the following specific commitments (Vera Institute of Justice, 2012b):

- commitment from the state executive and legislative leadership to support the pilot project with both policy and resources
- commitment from Departments of Public Safety that all reasonable measures would be taken to minimize and mitigate these actions to ensure that educational programming could proceed as planned
- commitment from the director of the state parole or postrelease community supervision agency and a detailed plan from the head of the supervision agency for how the agency would align its practices to support the education effort
- commitment from and cooperation of the participating community colleges and/ or community college system in the pilot state, specifically (1) certifying the credentials of corrections educators and the curricula used in corrections education programs for the purposes of granting credits to students for those courses after release; (2) signing articulation agreements with the corrections departments; (3) agreeing to provide tuition assistance to students when released; (4) offering academic counseling to incarcerated students before release; (5) offering courses taught by their staffs inside prisons; and (6) cooperating with mentoring and other support activities for previously incarcerated students on their campuses.

Furthermore, all stakeholders were asked to commit to cooperate with the evaluation of the Pathways Program. Specifically, each state was given incentive funding for the four-year pilot with a planned evaluation to be completed after sufficient outcome data could be collected to analyze the impact and outcomes of this demonstration project. Through a competitive selection process, the RAND Corporation, in partnership with RTI International, was chosen by Vera to evaluate the Pathways demonstration project. There were two phases to the evaluation. First, RAND and RTI completed a process evaluation that focused on the implementation of the in-prison component of the three Pathways pilot programs in Michigan, New Jersey, and North Carolina. This initial phase of the evaluation was funded by the Ford Foundation, the Sunshine Lady Foundation, the Open Society Foundations, the Bill and Melinda Gates Foundation, and the W. K. Kellogg Foundation (Vera Institute of Justice, 2012a).

The second phase of the evaluation was a process evaluation of the community component of North Carolina's Pathways Program to (1) document students' experiences as they returned to local communities to continue their education and (2) identify the factors that facilitated or hindered their ability to remain in the Pathways Program and earn a degree or credential. The Laughing Gull Foundation and Vera Institute of Justice provided funding to RAND and RTI International to conduct the process evaluation of the community component. Before discussing the specific objectives of the process evaluation, we provide some context on what North Carolina did prior to and after the Pathways Program.

Postsecondary Education in North Carolina's Prison System Prior to Pathways

Prior to the Pathways Program, individuals incarcerated in North Carolina were allowed to enroll in PSE correspondence programs offered by the University of North Carolina (UNC) system or other colleges and universities across the country.[7] NCDPS coordinated and paid for correspondence courses through UNC-Chapel Hill. Other types of correspondence courses and study release, for example, had to be approved by NCDPS but were paid for by family members or private donations.

PSE programs funded by the state were primarily CTE. The NCDPS Division of Adult Correction (DAC) (now known as the Division of Adult Corrections and Juvenile Justice) provided CTE and other education services to incarcerated individuals through partnerships with state and federal entities. For example, the DAC had a long-standing relationship with the North Carolina Community College System (NCCCS) in which the Prison Education Program (PEP) offered educational opportunities ranging from adult basic education to PSE courses taught by NCCCS instructors.

State legislation in 2009 and 2010 limited PSE programs in prison to an Associate of Applied Science (AAS) degree. Therefore, most PEP offerings prior to the Pathways Program were postsecondary vocational occupational extension classes that led to certificates of completion. The DAC also offered journeyman-level apprenticeships through the U.S. Department of Labor in conjunction with the NCCCS. The DAC offered a range of these workforce training courses in its 66 correctional facilities. In 2012, at the time of North Carolina's Pathways proposal application, NCCCS offered

---

[7] This summary is based on the North Carolina Department of Public Safety's (NCDPS's) 2012 proposal application for Pathways funding and a February 14, 2019, conference call with the NCDPS director of reentry programs and services.

68 different courses in the prison setting that were considered nonarticulating voca-tional classes. Courses included horticulture, food service, and construction trades, as well as advanced computer training. Any credits or credentials received by incarcerated students were provided at the time of their release from prison. Although students did not earn college credits that were applicable toward an award for these classes, partici-pation was reflected on their transcripts. Furthermore, the DAC and NCCCS had no articulation agreements.[8]

Before the Pathways Program, the DAC did not offer formal academic counseling and guidance to the incarcerated population. Instead, adult inmates could work with their assigned case managers to develop a case plan for their period of education. How-ever, although education was an area addressed by the case managers, their ability to offer focused academic or career guidance was limited by each case manager's knowl-edge and experience. Incarcerated students did not receive assistance with transferring PSE credits earned to another educational institution postrelease. Furthermore, case managers and probation and parole officers (PPOs) were not trained to offer assistance in academic counseling to students as they prepared for release. Finally, there was little reentry planning per se (e.g., preplanning, coordination, building of relationships) to facilitate the reentry process. Instead, it was up to the individual being released from prison to develop his or her own plan and determine his or her next steps, meaning that if an inmate was organized, he or she would have developed a reentry plan; otherwise, an individual was released from prison without any plan.

As we discuss in the next section, the Pathways Program addressed these limita-tions and was designed to expand and strengthen the PSE and reentry services available to individuals incarcerated in North Carolina's correctional system.

North Carolina's Pathways Program Design

The original design for North Carolina's Pathways pilot, which followed the model proposed in the request for proposals issued by the Vera Institute of Justice and devised by the funders of the Pathways initiative, is shown in Figure 1.1 and described in more detail in the following sections. Developing the logic model was part of the efforts by RAND and RTI in the original process evaluation. The initiative was led by the NCDPS Office of Reentry Programs and Services in collaboration with the NCCCS.

Inputs

NCDPS planned to use a variety of inputs (resources) to implement its Pathways ini-tiative, including its existing infrastructure and partnerships with NCCCS and local

---

[8]   An *articulation agreement* is a formal agreement between two or more colleges and universities—or, in this case, between NCDPS and NCCCS—that governs the transfer of credits for a specific academic program or degree.

Figure 1.1
North Carolina Pathways Program Logic Model

Inputs → In-Prison Implementation → Postrelease Implementation → Outcomes/Impacts

Inputs

Resources and Infrastructure

Preexisting infrastructure, facilities, and relationships in place as part of North Carolina's PEP

Pathways funding and other sources (e.g., Department of Corrections [DOC] and welfare funds)

In-prison resources:
- DOC staff, including state/prison education staff, case managers, regional program coordinators, and superintendents
- community college staff

Community resources:
- community college staff
- reentry council, including reentry coordinators, job placement specialists, and pathway navigators*
- community corrections
- other community resources (e.g., Joblink)

Pathways Program:
- program planning
- course structure and planning
- staff training
- partnership-building and stakeholder engagement

Academic model:
- academic and occupational training toward an AAS
- developmental education
- assessment-driven placement
- noninstructional supports
- classroom instruction enhanced by computer technology
- behavior management by students signing behavioral contract

Technical assistance:
- Vera staff and consultants

In-Prison Implementation

In-Prison Educational Activities
- developmental education**
- college programs resulting in a certificate, diploma, or degree
- adult: business administration, computer information technology (IT), and entrepreneurship
- youth: gaming/simulated IT

Academic and Instructional Supports
- enrollment management, including counseling on assessment results, orientation, and behavioral contract*
- tutoring*
- dedicated study hall*
- dedicated case managers*
- student cohorts*

Supplemental Services and Components
- participants living in shared quarters*
- computer training, access to computer lab and monitored/limited internet*
- trust-fund incentives for meeting performance goals*
- flexible visitation schedule and financial assistance for visiting families*

Prerelease Activities
- success team develops release plan*
- home planning and supports assessed
- Free Application for Federal Student Aid (FAFSA) and other assistance forms completed*
- counseling/advising on transcripts and articulation agreements*
- vital documents (e.g., identification) provided
- student package (e.g., laptop, bookbag, and other school supplies) provided*
- assigned parole officer meets with participants*

Postrelease Implementation

Outputs: Participants Reenter the Community Exhibiting the Following:
- enrollment and persistence through in-prison Pathways Program*
- obtainment of certification and possibly diploma
- engagement with reentry council to set up postrelease activities
- enrollment in community college courses

Postrelease Activities
- structured college courses and support services*
- reentry support through a council, including reentry coordinators and job placement specialists, Pathways navigators*
- dedicated parole officer to facilitate group supervision and other group activities*
- financial support for reentry needs, including college tuition, housing, and childcare*

* Indicates that this service was available only to Pathways participants

** Indicates limited availability to non-Pathways participants

Outcomes/Impacts

Outcomes
- college enrollment
- college completion
- obtainment of certificates, diplomas, and degrees
- employment (part-time or full-time)
- reductions in recidivism; fewer community supervision violations

Individual and Family Impact
- successful family reunification
- better perception of DOC and the corrections system
- reduced intergenerational poverty by improving education of undereducated population

Correctional System Impact
- inmates: increased motivation to earn a GED and join Pathways
- safer prison environment
- stronger community transition process
- education fully integrated into release planning/preparation
- more-efficient correctional education programs

Societal Impacts
- reduced criminal justice costs
- reduced crime and increased public safety
- improved quality of life in neighborhoods impacted by crime and incarceration
- skilled workforce
- taxpaying citizens

Prerelease Activities
- policy, funding, and reentry environment
- community socioeconomic characteristics
- family characteristics and other supports
- student characteristics
- community support services (housing, treatment, counseling)
- community colleges
- state course articulation agreements
- labor market and employers

reentry councils (LRCs). North Carolina received $1 million in incentive funding to implement Pathways and was required to provide an overall match of at least 25 percent.[9] Designated in-kind resources included assistance from state-level staff at NCDPS and NCCCS and staff in the participating prisons (e.g., prison education staff, case managers, regional program coordinators, and superintendents) and release communities (e.g., community college staff and LRCs).

Other planned inputs included the design of North Carolina's Pathways Program, which aimed to offer PSE, instructional supports, and noninstructional supports to 150 eligible incarcerated persons within two years of release from prison and through the first two years after their release. North Carolina identified the following eligibility criteria for individuals to be accepted into the program: They must have a high school credential, be assessed college ready using the Accuplacer or ASSET assessments, be within two years of release, have no gang involvement, and be willing to transfer to a designated Pathways facility and sign a behavioral contract.[10]

As one of three Pathways pilot sites, North Carolina also received technical assistance from the Vera Institute of Justice and opportunities to engage with and learn from the other two Pathways pilot sites (Michigan and New Jersey) and stakeholders.

Implementation
As illustrated in Figure 1.1, the original design for implementation of the North Carolina Pathways Program encompassed in-prison and postrelease activities.

In-Prison Activities
While incarcerated, Pathways students would have the option of earning a certificate (12–18 semester credit courses), an Associate in General Education, or an AAS degree. Regardless of which credential a participant chose to pursue, each program was structured to focus on general education courses that would result in credits that could be transferred to PSE programs postrelease. However, participants would not be permitted to earn higher-level degrees while incarcerated because of a state law limiting postsecondary programs in state prisons to the terminal AAS degree. Additional supports made available to participants in prison were developmental precredit instruction in English and math, tutoring, space and supervision for study hall or study groups, dedicated case managers, and computer training and restricted internet access.[11] North Carolina also offered the following supplemental services: a separate housing unit to

---

[9]   The overall match of at least 25 percent was made up of 15 percent in the form of a cash match (from public and/or private sources) and 10 percent in-kind resources to be distributed over the four years of the demonstration project.

[10] Some of these eligibility requirements (e.g., scores on assessments) were later relaxed during the selection process to ensure that enough students were recruited.

[11] Restricted internet access in prisons uses routers and firewalls that permit only certain internet content to come through the system.

facilitate the participants' educational experience outside the classroom, incentive payments for meeting performance goals and to offset wages Pathways students would have otherwise earned through prison jobs, and a flexible visitation schedule for the students' families.

NCDPS also structured the Pathways Program to include "success" teams made up of the Pathways navigator, the reentry council coordinator, a PPO, and a job placement specialist. These success teams were to meet with participants at least once in the six months prior to release to develop a transition plan, review the process for applying for financial aid and enrolling in college, and discuss housing options and other supports available in the community.

Postrelease Activities

The goal of the North Carolina Pathways Program was for students to continue their educational coursework postrelease and be provided with the reentry and other services needed to support their educational persistence and attainment. As illustrated in Figure 1.1, plans for postrelease implementation included outputs (products from the in-prison activities) and postrelease activities. In terms of postrelease outputs, NCDPS envisioned that Pathways students would reenter the community with a certificate (12–18 semester credit courses) and/or a diploma in general education prior to enrolling in a community or other college to earn a more advanced PSE credential. Postrelease activities would include college courses; financial support for college tuition (either through assistance in applying for federal student aid or assistance with barriers to receiving financial aid through scholarships made possible with Pathways funding[12]); and assistance with housing, childcare, transportation, and employment.

North Carolina also identified the following three release communities and community colleges for the Pathways students:

- Greenville/Pitt County: Pitt Community College
- Charlotte/Mecklenburg County: Central Piedmont Community College (CPCC)
- Asheville/Buncombe County: Asheville-Buncombe Technical Community College (AB-Tech).

The plan was for students to be placed on a specialized Pathways caseload of a dedicated PPO who was supportive of education, who was familiar with the Pathways Program, and who had a strong relationship with the LRC.

---

[12] Such barriers include prior default on federal student loans, failure to register for Selective Service, and felony drug convictions. The time required to clear up these challenges led to the decision to supplement with Pathways funds in order to get these students enrolled in college.

Outcomes and Impacts

The logic model shown in Figure 1.1 indicates that NCDPS hoped that Pathways participants would achieve the following short-term and medium-term outcomes: college enrollment, persistence, and completion; attainment of certificates, diplomas, and degrees; gainful employment, either part-time or full-time, and increased earnings; and reductions in recidivism, including fewer community supervision violations and instances of misconduct.

NCDPS also envisioned having an impact on participating students and their families, the correctional system, and society. At the individual and family level, NCDPS wanted Pathways students to develop increased self-esteem and a sense of hope, including reenvisioning their future. Intended long-term impacts at the individual and family level included family reunification and stability and a reduction in intergenerational poverty by improving the education of an undereducated population.

At the correctional system level, desired impacts included that education programs within prison would become more efficient and fully integrated into reentry planning and that education would become a valued part of the culture for staff and inmates. NCDPS also hoped that the Pathways Program would serve as an example to other inmates and help motivate incarcerated individuals who were not involved in the program to focus on their education. In addition, by changing the culture, NCDPS hoped that Pathways would help correctional staff see the value of prison-based PSE programming. Finally, at the correctional system level, there was a recognition that participation in Pathways may lead to a safer prison environment, with reductions in incidents and misconduct.

At the societal level, NCDPS identified developing a skilled workforce and more tax-paying citizens as positive impacts. In addition, in the long run, it hoped to improve the quality of life in neighborhoods affected by crime, reduce crime, and improve public safety while reducing criminal justice costs.

Individual and Contextual Factors

In addition, as illustrated in Figure 1.1, NCDPS anticipated that several individual and contextual factors may affect Pathways implementation and the students' ability to remain in the program and earn a credential postrelease. Such factors included the policy, funding, and reentry environment. For example, as noted earlier, state law limited Pathways students to an AAS degree program while incarcerated. North Carolina also had limited reentry capabilities and, therefore, planned to use its Pathways funding to strengthen newly established LRCs in the three designated release communities. It was also planned for the LRCs to use the funds to customize services based on the students' needs and available community resources, including employment opportunities, transportation, housing, and counseling services. Other anticipated variations among the three communities, which we will discuss later in this report, included the community staff's approach to providing the Pathways students with educational opportunities and the proximity and layout of the community college campuses.

Finally, as shown in Figure 1.1, NCDPS identified other factors that may affect Pathways implementation, including the students' characteristics and families. For example, students with children may feel pressure to decide between focusing on their education and focusing on parental responsibilities.

Study Objectives

The objective of our evaluation was to examine the implementation of the North Carolina Pathways Program's in-prison and community components. Specifically, we were interested in how the in-prison program was designed and implemented; the eligibility requirements for, and the selection of, the Pathways participants; the funding and resources available; the community colleges and other stakeholders engaged; the factors that facilitated or hindered program implementation and students' participation; the adjustments made; and the lessons learned. We also were interested in understanding the experiences of North Carolina Pathways students as they transitioned back into the community, including what reentry supports were critical, what factors facilitated or hindered continuation or completion of their educational programs, adjustments made, and lessons learned.

The overarching Pathways demonstration project was the first data collection we are aware of that focused specifically on understanding the reentry process for students beginning PSE while incarcerated and continuing their coursework upon release, with the ultimate goal of achieving an associate's degree or other credentials. This study comes at a critical time, as interest in expanding PSE for justice-involved populations at the state and federal levels grows. RAND and RTI were able to capture the students' experiences and insights about the reentry process, the factors that facilitated or hindered their transitions, and the academic and support services available. We also documented how students navigated the college transition process and the reunification with their families. These lessons learned through North Carolina's Pathways Program have national implications.

Study Approach

We used a multimethod approach to evaluate the in-prison and community components of North Carolina's Pathways Program. See Appendixes B and C for the consent protocols and discussion guides used in this study. In this section, we briefly summarize the methods for each phase of the evaluation.

In-Prison Component Evaluation

As noted earlier, the evaluation of the in-prison component of Pathways was funded by a consortium of funders that supported the overall demonstration project—the Ford Foundation, the Sunshine Lady Foundation, the Open Society Foundations, the Bill and Melinda Gates Foundation, and the W. K. Kellogg Foundation. With respect to the in-prison component, we conducted two rounds of site visits to North Carolina in spring and fall 2014, which allowed us to collect data at two points in time—first, when the Pathways Program had been under way for several months and then again nine months into program implementation. Using a semistructured interview protocol, we conducted in-person interviews with a range of stakeholders involved in planning for and implementing North Carolina's Pathways Program. At the correctional facility level, stakeholders included the superintendent and assistant superintendent, correctional supervisors, education staff, college instructors, and the Pathways team; at the headquarters level, stakeholders included state corrections officials and the Pathways administrator. We conducted a total of 25 interviews. The interviews focused on Pathways Program planning, including the different program components, course structure, eligibility requirements, and selection of Pathways participants; academic and instructional supports; and noninstructional supports. The interviews also covered staff training and development, funding and resources available to the program, partnership-building and stakeholder engagement, factors that facilitated or hindered the implementation of Pathways, strategies to mitigate challenges encountered, and lessons learned. We began each interview by reviewing the informed consent protocol following institutional review board (IRB) protocols and requested permission to audio-record these discussions; all the interviewees agreed to this request.

In addition, we conducted two sets of focus groups with a total of 13 Pathways students who were in the in-prison program during October 2014. To select the focus group participants, we sent information about the purpose of the evaluation and the focus group discussions in advance and asked for Pathways students to indicate whether they would be interested in participating in the discussion. We used a semistructured discussion guide to facilitate these discussions, which covered the following topics: (1) motivation for applying to Pathways; (2) educational goals and how the program may have helped them in meeting those goals; (3) early experiences with the Pathways Program, including coursework and instructional and noninstructional support needs; (4) perceptions about the program's strength and weaknesses; (5) plans for continuing their PSE upon release from prison; (6) views about support needs; and (7) their advice for improving the program. All focus group discussions were conducted in a private classroom setting where no correctional staff or program staff were present. We began each session by reviewing the informed consent protocol as specified by IRB protocol. To protect the identity and confidentiality of the participants, we did not audio-record these discussions, and we assigned a numeric ID to each participant so that no names were recorded in the handwritten notes.

Community Component Evaluation

The evaluation of the community component of the Pathways Program was funded by the Laughing Gull Foundation and the Vera Institute of Justice. We conducted two site visits to Greenville and one site visit each to Asheville and Charlotte—the three designated release communities to evaluate the community component of Pathways. We used semistructured discussion guides to facilitate the interviews and focus group discussions that were conducted in 2016 and 2017. Depending on when an individual had been released from prison, the timing of these conversations occurred either early in their release or up to six months after they had been out in the community. Several individuals participated in both the in-prison and community focus group discussions; otherwise, these conversations represented a cross-section of Pathways students who were out in the community.

We conducted in-depth interviews with Pathways Program staff, reentry staff, community college staff, housing providers, and PPOs involved in the community component of the North Carolina Pathways Program. In total, we interviewed 37 individuals at the state and local levels. The logic model in Figure 1.1 guided our discussions, which focused on postrelease implementation activities and outputs. Specifically, using a semistructured discussion guide, we collected information about the design and implementation of the Pathways Program at the local level; academic, instructional, and noninstructional supports provided out in the community; reentry services provided by the LRCs and the role of the Pathways navigator; funding and resources; partnership-building and stakeholder engagement at the local level; and what adjustments were made to the postrelease community component of the program to address specific issues as they arose. We were also interested in interviewees' views about factors that facilitated or hindered implementation of the community component of the Pathways Program, strategies to mitigate challenges encountered, their overall assessment of the successes and challenges, and lessons learned. In addition, we conducted state-level interviews with NCDPS correctional education staff responsible for designing, implementing, and overseeing the Pathways Program. This allowed us to get a higher-level perspective of the overall approach North Carolina took to the Pathways Program, stakeholders' assessments of critical factors and challenges, adjustments made, lessons learned, and future plans for the program. We began each interview with a review of the consent form that followed IRB protocols and requested permission to audio-record the interview; all interviewees agreed to this request.

To obtain the perspective of Pathways participants who had returned to local communities, we conducted in-depth focus groups with Pathways students; where this was infeasible, we conducted telephone interviews with students who dropped out of the program to capture their experiences and assessments of the community component of the Pathways Program. As noted earlier, several of the participants in the focus group discussions for the community component also had participated in conversations as part of the earlier evaluation of the in-prison component. In total, we spoke with 38 current or former Pathways students—13 in Asheville, 16 in Charlotte, and nine in Greenville. The logic model shown in Figure 1.1 informed the development of the focus group discussion guide and interview protocol, specifically with regard to the postrelease experiences of the Pathways students. To select the focus group participants, we sent information about the purpose of the evaluation and the focus group discussions in advance and asked for Pathways students to indicate whether they would be interested in participating in the discussion. All interviews and focus group discussions were conducted in a private setting, with no program staff, PPOs, reentry navigators, or college instructors present. We began each session by reviewing the oral consent form that followed IRB protocols. We also requested permission to audio-record the focus group discussions and interviews for note-taking purposes; all but one student agreed to this request. The focus group discussions and interviews with Pathways students focused on their experiences with returning to the community, enrolling in a community-based college program, the services and supports they received, their experiences in finding employment and housing, and the factors that facilitated or hindered their transition to the community and influenced their decisions about whether to continue in their educational programs. We also asked what advice they would give to other formerly incarcerated students interested in pursuing higher education programs and asked for their overall assessment of the Pathways Program and recommendations for how it might be improved. In addition, where possible, we interviewed students who had dropped out of the program to get their perspectives on factors that influenced their decisions, their assessments of the program, their educational plans, and recommendations for improving the program.

Analysis

We qualitatively analyzed the interview and focus group data. To analyze these data, two researchers reviewed the notes to identify general themes. The audio recordings were used to correct and fill in gaps in our notes. We then compared individual reviews and reached agreement on the key themes that emerged. We used a cutting-and-sorting technique to identify specific themes with respect to the staff interviews and the Pathways student interviews and focus group discussions. We identified themes that were similar or different across the release communities and lessons learned. We also identified quotes or expressions that summarized key discussion points.

Study Limitations

We were unable to conduct in-person interviews with the few North Carolina Pathways students who were reincarcerated during the study period; thus, our evaluation is missing their perspectives.

Where possible, we tried to interview or conduct focus group discussions with the full cohort of Pathways students currently in the three reentry communities at the time of our site visits. This was not always possible because some students were unavailable to participate in the evaluation because of conflicts with their work or school schedules, because they had moved out of the area, or because they had declined to participate in the evaluation study. To the extent that this occurred, we are missing their perspectives.

Finally, it was not within the scope of this project to quantitatively analyze the outcomes of the North Carolina Pathways Program shown in Figure 1.1. However, we do offer our qualitative assessment of the short-term outcomes of the program identified as part of this study.

Roadmap for This Report

In Chapter Two, we summarize our findings from the evaluation of the in-prison component of the North Carolina Pathways Program from the analysis we conducted, and we present our findings for the community component of the program in Chapter Three. In Chapter Four, we summarize the key conclusions and lessons learned across both analyses and provide our recommendations for stakeholders from other states that might be interested in implementing college programs for this population based on North Carolina's experience. In Appendix A, we present an overview of the overall Pathways demonstration project. Appendixes B and C include the interview protocols and discussion guides used for the evaluation of the in-prison and community components of the North Carolina Pathways Program, respectively.

CHAPTER TWO

The North Carolina Pathways Program's In-Prison Component

In order to understand how the community component of the Pathways Program unfolded, it is important to examine how the in-prison component was designed and implemented, including student selection, recruitment and enrollment, courses and other services provided, adjustments made, and lessons learned. The experiences of Pathways students in prison help set the context for understanding the community component of the Pathways Program, which is discussed in Chapter Three.

North Carolina's Pathways Program Structure

The Pathways Program was housed within the NCDPS Office of Reentry Services and Programs (formerly known as the Division of Rehabilitative Services and Programs), and the director was responsible for its statewide implementation.

In 2012, the following six correctional facilities out of North Carolina's 66 prison facilities were designated as facility sites for the Pathways Program:[1]

1. Avery-Mitchell Correctional Institution (medium security, male population)
2. Craggy Correctional Center (formerly Buncombe Correctional Center; minimum and medium security, male population)[2]
3. Mountain View Correctional Institution (close/medium security, male population)
4. Albemarle Correctional Institution (medium security, male population)
5. Pamlico Correctional Institution (medium security, male population)

---

[1] In North Carolina, no single county receives more than 10 percent of exits from prison in a given year. NCDPS selected three counties that typically had high reentry rates for offenders. Of the 26,685 exits from prison between July 2011 and June 2012, Pitt (Greenville; 2.3 percent), Mecklenburg (Charlotte; 6.1 percent), and Buncombe (Asheville; 2.5 percent) counties were among the top five reentry locations (NCDPS, 2012).

[2] Craggy Correctional Center, located near Asheville, is a medium/minimum security prison for adult males. In March 2014, it consolidated with Buncombe Correctional Center to house a population of adult males in medium and minimum custody (NCDPS, undated[a]).

6. Swannanoa Correctional Center for Women (minimum security, female population).

North Carolina's state policy limited inmates to earning only an AAS degree, which was considered a terminal degree. To address this, the NCCCS, in collaboration with NCDPS, identified courses that not only applied to an AAS degree but also could serve as the core curriculum for other degrees once the students were released and no longer barred from obtaining other types of degrees.

The AAS track was to operate at Avery-Mitchell, Mountain View, Albemarle, Craggy, and Pamlico correctional centers for adult males in medium security. The following community colleges provided traditional, in-person classes for the Pathways Program: Mayland Community College conducted courses for Pathways at Avery-Mitchell and Mountain View; Stanley Community College served Albemarle; AB-Tech served Craggy; and Pamlico Community College served Pamlico. Male inmate students needing developmental courses were to be housed at either Avery-Mitchell or Mountain View facilities to complete these courses. Then, they would be transferred to Albemarle or Pamlico prison facilities to participate in core technical and general education courses toward the AAS degree.

In North Carolina, the female inmates were housed at Swannanoa. AB-Tech conducted the Pathways college courses offered at this facility. These offerings included developmental courses and core technical and general education courses needed for the AAS degree.

Prior Educational Experiences of the Pathways Students
The Pathways students varied in their educational experiences prior to incarceration. Many had some college before they were incarcerated and were interested in continuing their college education. To give a sense of the type of variation in their educational experience prior to incarceration, of those students who participated in our focus group discussions or interviews for both the in-prison and community components,

- seven students had dropped out of high school and had not earned their GED[3]
- seven students had completed high school or had their GED (but no college)
- ten students had completed high school or had their GED and had some college coursework
- two had finished their associate's degrees
- two had certifications in a trade program
- two had taken correspondence courses from local community colleges or four-year universities.

---

[3] To give a sense of how this compares with the rest of the prison population, in 2011 there were 27,770 admissions to prison. Twenty-four percent of incarcerated individuals reported having completed 12th grade or higher (NCDPS, 2012).

In addition, prior to enrolling in Pathways, several students had taken other educational or vocational training classes while in prison. In general, they used this time to complete their GEDs and/or to take whatever vocational training or CTE programs were offered and available in the correctional facility where they were located. While incarcerated and before enrollment in Pathways, students were commonly participating in as many programs as they could, suggesting that many were motivated to further their education before joining Pathways. For example, of those students who participated in our focus group discussions or interviews,

- seven students had earned their GEDs while incarcerated
- three students were teaching assistants
- two students had earned computer information technology (IT) certificates
- two students took college correspondence courses
- 11 students had taken a variety of CTE or vocational training courses prior to enrollment in Pathways, including courses in heating, ventilation, and air conditioning (HVAC); electrical wiring; commercial cleaning; welding; furniture upholstery; horticulture; food services and culinary arts; carpentry; and masonry.[4]

Student Selection Criteria, Recruitment, and Enrollment

Table 2.1 shows the original selection criteria for North Carolina's Pathways Program, which followed the Pathways Program's two-years-in and two-years-out model. Potential students were required to have at least a high school equivalency diploma, and the program staff reviewed applicants' test scores (e.g., using the Test of Adult Basic Education [TABE]) to determine college readiness. Although its Pathways Program was being offered in only a few correctional facilities, NCDPS recruited and enrolled students statewide by sharing information about the program with all incarcerated individuals who met the basic eligibility criteria. This meant that selected students agreed to be transferred to one of the Pathways correctional facilities. They also agreed to be released to one of three release communities—Asheville, Charlotte, or Greenville)[5]—and to sign a behavioral contract.[6]

---

[4] These categories could overlap; for example, one student could earn his or her GED and take other courses.

[5] The three release communities were selected based on the number of estimated eligible inmates for the Pathways Program who were planning to exit to these locations in 2012. In addition, the three communities were selected because of the number of institutions of higher learning in these communities and the availability of community-based resources and service providers that could support an LRC (NCDPS, 2012).

[6] The behavioral contract detailed the requirements of program participation. The contract stated that the Pathways participant would agree to participate in the program for the time remaining on their prison sentence; to enroll in an AAS degree program upon their release from prison or seek full-time employment; to attend classes;

Table 2.1
North Carolina Pathways Program's Selection Criteria, Recruitment Procedures, and Enrollment Procedures

Selection Criteria	
High school credential	Required
Release date	Within two years of release
Must release to designated communities	Required
Classification or sentencing requirements	Low-level offender (minimum or medium); no sexual predators or active gang members
Misconducts	No active gang members at time of application
TABE tested	Required
Additional assessments	Beta IQ and Wide Range Achievement Test (WRAT)
Transfer to designated correctional facilities	Required (if not located in one of three Pathway facilities, students agree to be transferred)
Recruitment Procedures	
Screening	Query performed at the state level
Orientation	Conducted by NCDPS staff
Application	Required; scored using rubric
Enrollment Procedures	
Behavioral contract	Required
Transfers	Required (six correctional facilities)
Placement exam	Required
Prerequisite class	No requirements
Developmental education	Available if needed
Other enrollment procedures	No requirements

SOURCE: Data were provided by NCDPS.

In addition, students were offered a variety of incentives to participate in the Pathways Program. These included phone cards for meeting weekly performance goals and help in offsetting wages they would have otherwise earned through prison jobs sacrificed to enroll in school full-time.[7] Pathways participants were eligible to receive a $5 incentive upon enrollment in classes each semester. They also were eligible to receive end-of-semester incentives in the form of a finals study break (e.g., movie, pizza

---

to complete all assignments in a timely manner; to not commit any major infractions (any Class A, specified Class B, or any combination of three or more infractions within a 30-day period); to maintain an overall grade point average (GPA) of at least 2.2; and to abide by any postrelease and/or probation conditions after exiting from prison (NCDPS, 2014).

[7]   The Pathways Performance Incentive process was based on weekly progress reports from the community college instructors who completed an incentive roster for each class they taught on a weekly basis. The instructor rated each Pathways student using a letter grade from A to D in the following areas: class attendance, class participation, class preparation, and assignments (NCDPS, 2014).

party) and were awarded a monetary incentive based on their semester final GPAs.[8] Other incentives included a flexible visitation schedule for the students' families and gas cards to help pay for their travel costs.

Table 2.2 summarizes the statistics for how the in-prison component of the North Carolina Pathways Program unfolded. A total of 1,513 inmates were recruited (of that number, 152 individuals self-referred to the program). Of those who were recruited, 1,043 applied to the program and 201 were accepted.

To get a sense of reasons for not being accepted into the program, among the first cohort, 197 of the 333 individuals who applied in fall 2013 were rejected for the following reasons: 58 individuals had placement scores that were inadequate; 71 individuals' exit dates did not meet the criteria for participation in the program; 18 individuals failed to maintain eligibility for the program; ten individuals were rejected because of lack of program slots at the time of their application and were either wait-listed or encouraged to participate in other educational programs offered; two individuals were randomly assigned to the control group; and 38 individuals failed to meet other eligibility criteria.

Over the course of the in-prison component of the Pathways Program, a total of 3,750 credits and 259 certificates were earned by Pathways students.

In-Prison Educational Activities, Supports, and Prerelease Statistics

North Carolina's Pathways Program allowed students to select from the following two-year AAS degree programs: business administration, computer IT, and entrepreneurship. NCDPS and its community college partners selected these programs because they included core courses that could easily be transferred to other college programs postrelease. College and career counseling also were provided to the Pathways students.

Table 2.2
Statistics for the In-Prison Component of the North Carolina Pathways Program, as of August 2018

Statistic	Number
Inmates recruited	1,513
Inmates that applied	1,043
Total credits earned	3,750
Total certificates earned	259

SOURCE: Data were provided by NCDPS.

---

[8]   This award was based on the official grades earned for credit by the student. A $15 deposit was made for a GPA between 3.75 and 4.00; a $7.50 deposit was made for a GPA between 2.51 and 3.74; a $3.50 deposit was made for a GPA between 2.00 and 2.50; and no deposit was made for a GPA of 1.99 or lower (NCDPS, 2014).

It became clear early on that more students than originally anticipated based on their educational backgrounds needed developmental education courses. Most North Carolina Pathways students were placed in developmental courses at the beginning of their participation in the program to address reading, writing, and other deficits to prepare them to take college courses. After completion of their developmental courses, they began to take their curriculum courses.[9]

In addition to the Pathways curriculum courses, other educational programs offered to Pathways students included study release, in which an individual inmate could participate in an academic or vocational training/CTE program away from the correctional facility. Study release was utilized for a handful of students. In terms of computer training, NCDPS offered its students limited internet access and a keyboarding course in at least one of its participating facilities. Students were encouraged to form study groups and were provided with time in the computer lab and access to a study room and tutors.

North Carolina housed its Pathways students in the same living quarters with the goal of creating a more learning-friendly environment, although this approach was eventually dropped by one of the correctional facilities because students were perceived by the staff as abusing this privilege.

North Carolina's Pathways Program was set up so that most students would be able to earn a college certificate while incarcerated, which included 12–18 semester credit courses and some major courses. Table 2.2 indicates that a total of 3,750 credits were earned during the in-prison component of the program. Certificates earned by North Carolina Pathways students while in prison were in entrepreneurship, business administration, computer IT, and developmental coursework completion. No student earned an AAS degree while incarcerated.

Prerelease from the In-Prison Component of the Pathways Program

For the in-prison component of the North Carolina Pathways Program, a total of 201 individuals had exited the in-prison component as of August 2018; of those, 165 participated in the program postrelease.

North Carolina expected its Pathways students to continue their education or to work full-time once they were back in the community. Prerelease, a relatively small number of students had completed a college application and were accepted by a college, had obtained transcripts from current and former colleges, had submitted a North Carolina financial aid application, or had submitted a Free Application for Federal

---

[9]   Some students also took continuing education courses.

Student Aid (FAFSA) application.[10] This suggests that applying to community colleges and submitting financial aid forms would occur largely after students' release from prison. This in turn had implications for the type of educational support Pathways students needed postrelease and the roles and responsibilities of the Pathways navigator and college staff, as we discuss further in Chapter Three. Postrelease, 66 students submitted applications for admission to community colleges and all 66 were accepted.

As part of the prerelease phase of the program, Pathways participants met with a "success team" comprising a case manager from the LRC and a representative of community supervision (PPO or chief PPO, as needed). The success team met with the student at least once or twice six months prior to his or her release from prison to develop a transition plan to facilitate continuation of the student's educational process after he or she returned to the community (NCDPS, 2014). As part of the prerelease planning process, and depending on their needs, students were referred to such services as employment, housing, transportation, mental health treatment, substance abuse treatment, and family and childcare services.[11] As we discuss in Chapter Three, the range of services needed underscored the reentry challenges that many Pathways students faced as they transitioned back into the community.

Adjustments Made and Lessons Learned

In this section, we highlight the key adjustments made to the in-prison component of the North Carolina Pathways Program and lessons learned. Some of the adjustments made had implications for the community component of the program, as we discuss in Chapter Three.

Selection, Recruitment, and Enrollment Processes
In the first year, North Carolina experienced some challenges with its selection, recruitment, and enrollment processes and made adjustments as needed. North Carolina had less than six months from the time of the award of the grant to the deadline for stand-

[10] For example, statistics from May 2016 indicate that prerelease, only eight students had completed a college application and been accepted to college, 12 students had transcripts obtained from current or former colleges, 17 students had submitted a North Carolina financial aid application, and 19 students had completed a FAFSA application.

[11] For non-Pathways students, there were no prerelease plans or referrals to reentry support services. In terms of transition services, Pathways students were offered a variety of other correctional programs, including, for example, community volunteer leave, where inmates are allowed to attend activities in the local community; home leave to enable individuals nearing their release from prison to reestablish family relationships and experience community socialization in preparation for their transition back into the community; use of the Transitional Aftercare Network (TAN), a statewide network of volunteers, churches. and faith-based ministries that assists ex-offenders in their transition back into their families, communities, and workforce; and other programs. See the NCDPS website for a description of its educational and other programs (NCDPS, undated[b]).

ing up its program.[12] The limited planning time to get its program up and running meant that NCDPS was learning as it rolled out the program. For example, the Pathways staff learned early on that family played a key role in the decisionmaking process for some of the applicants. During the first round of orientation, the North Carolina Pathways staff provided potential applicants with time to talk with their families in advance about whether they should apply to the program. Some of the potential applicants decided not to apply because family members (especially those with children) did not want them to move to another facility farther away. Other family members expressed a preference for the individual to have a work assignment that would enable him or her to send money home.

Student recruitment and selection were resource-intensive and time-intensive processes, and adjustments had to be made throughout to accommodate unexpected issues. North Carolina relaxed its selection criteria in order to get a sufficient pool of individuals eligible to apply to the program. As part of the application process, the North Carolina Pathways team also learned that it was important to place education holds on potential Pathways participants (i.e., so that an individual would not be transferred to another correctional facility or promoted to minimum custody)[13] during the application process or risk losing some individuals who wanted to be in the program but were in the process of being moved to another correctional facility.

Despite North Carolina's extensive screening processes, not all selected students assimilated well into the program in the first year, and a few left the program for personal reasons or misconduct (e.g., testing positive for drugs). As noted by one student, eligible candidates need to be told that they should not enroll in the program if they are not serious about obtaining an education: "You can't come in here and skate by." Similarly, a facility staff member said that she wished that a better interview process had been established to ensure that the students selected for the program were the right fit.

In-Prison Educational Activities and Supports
The complexity of putting into place a comprehensive program like Pathways and implementing it in multiple facilities, as well as working with local colleges and universities, required a full-time (or near full-time) commitment from the state's program lead. North Carolina hired a full-time Pathways Program staff member to take on many of the responsibilities of the Pathways Program administrator (who had other administrative responsibilities).

---

[12] Of the three states that participated in the Pathways Program, New Jersey had a preexisting program that it used for Pathways and was selected first. North Carolina was selected second. Michigan was selected last and, like North Carolina, had only a few months of planning time.

[13] Some students agreed to stay in medium custody to remain in the program because NCDPS had limited program slots in the various facilities.

Some of the incentives initially promised to Pathways students did not come to fruition. For example, in order to alleviate students' concerns about transferring to a Pathways-designated facility farther from their families, students were told that their families would receive gas cards. However, NCDPS ultimately was unable to provide families with these cards because of state procurement laws. Instead, NCDPS replaced the cards with an additional payment so that the students could purchase more phone time to maintain contact with family.

Although North Carolina's goal was to provide its Pathways students with time and appropriate space for studying, space limitations at some correctional facilities made this goal difficult to achieve. The amount of time students had in the computer lab to complete their homework assignments was somewhat limited because of space issues and scheduling conflicts (e.g., other education programs need access to the computer lab). In addition, providing students in North Carolina with restricted internet access created some security issues. For example, when access was first provided, email communication with college instructors not affiliated with the program was inadvertently made available to incarcerated students. As soon as the problem was discovered, the ability to email those instructors was removed. Although this issue and others were resolved, there were some misgivings among corrections staff, who felt that adopting the internet should have been done more slowly or not at all.

As noted earlier, North Carolina's state policy limited inmates to earning only an AAS degree, which was considered a terminal degree. As discussed in the next chapter, some Pathways students ended up changing their majors upon returning to local communities.

Funding

The full-time equivalent (FTE) funding structure of North Carolina's community colleges added a layer of complexity to how prison-based programs were funded. Specifically, because the funding did not cover start-up costs, other funding sources were used. Finding ways to make this funding structure work for both the community college system and NCDPS required both sides to be accommodating and innovative, especially because other prison-based education programs in North Carolina had a different funding structure (e.g., teachers were paid regardless of the number of seats filled).

Furthermore, prison-based education programs define their school year differently than do community colleges because incarcerated students typically have more time to complete courses than students on the outside. Also, creating student cohorts in the prison setting to comply with the community college FTE structure was challenging because the Pathways students in prison were typically at different educational levels.

Educating Staff and Students on the Pathways Program

It was important to get participating correctional facilities' staff on board, from the superintendents and assistant superintendents to the correctional officers and the facility-based educational staff. Although North Carolina's Pathways administrator did considerable outreach early on, educating staff was an ongoing process to continually reinforce the program's goals and structure. It required being as transparent and detailed as possible with both staff and students to avoid misinformation. It was common for the Pathways students and facility staff to have different understandings or interpretations of the program. For example, many of the students who had transferred to other correctional facilities to be part of the Pathways Program viewed their transfers as a sacrifice that should be respected and rewarded (particularly if they had to transfer from a minimum-security to a medium-security prison). But some facility staff felt that the students should just be grateful to be in the program. These differing views created some tension between the two groups. Program administrators at times found it challenging to accommodate students' education and study needs without making them feel as though they were privileged (e.g., different from other inmates) and above facility rules. A few of the students were perceived as having taken advantage of the facility staff's lack of understanding of the program. For example, in one of North Carolina's facilities, students told facility staff that the state administrator wanted the students to have more accommodations to support their ability to study for their classes than that being provided. The state administrator ultimately had to assure the facility staff that this was not true—all inmates had to comply with prison rules and constraints, regardless of their enrollment in the Pathways Program.

Support for Pathways varied from facility to facility in part because each facility has its own organizational culture and places different values on education programs. For example, a group of students took developmental courses for Pathways at one facility and were moved to another facility for the college-level coursework. The students described notable differences between the two prisons and how the education program was valued by the facility leadership and custody staff. They also commented that the quality of instruction was different. Although these differences affected the students' views of facility staff and instructors and feelings of support, the students' overall impression of and commitment to the program did not appear to change.

Some students and staff in North Carolina's facilities and colleges also reported feeling that insufficient time had been allotted for them to fully understand the program's requirements and expectations before it began. As one student noted, the initial description of the program was vague, but he decided to take a leap of faith because "free education is always good."

The state administrator also discovered that the Pathways students often were asking the college instructors questions the instructors were not prepared or trained to answer (e.g., career advice). The college instructors had to be reminded to answer only education-related questions and avoid agreeing to what might seem like innocuous requests.

Finally, North Carolina used education holds to ensure that Pathways students were able to complete their in-prison programs without being transferred to other facilities mid-stream. This meant that, in some cases, students had to agree to remain in medium custody even though they were eligible to be moved to minimum custody.

Corrections Leadership, Correctional Officers, and Facility Education Staff

The Pathways Program was embraced by the state's central leadership. This support helped set the tone that rehabilitation, and the Pathways Program in particular, was a priority. For example, a senior state administrator in North Carolina noted that Pathways needed state-level support for it to "transfer well" to the facilities. He explained that managing across many facilities can be challenging; as a result, unless senior leaders continually show their support for the program, it is not going to be taken seriously by custody staff.

Although the state leadership sets the tone for the state, facility superintendents are the personification of the correctional facilities. It was their responsibility to hold custody staff accountable for making the program work. The most common question and concern administrators had to address was how the program was being funded. Why should inmates be receiving an education when custody staff members cannot afford to send their children to college? The fact that outside foundations were paying for the program made it more palatable. Also, the administrators emphasized how the program would help with prison safety and that the Pathways students typically are not security risks because they are nearing release. Several administrators noted that when custody staff members saw the students' college-level work, they realized that many of the students were taking this opportunity seriously.

Some custody staff were very committed to the program. These staff members either had asked or had been recruited by the superintendent to supervise classroom space or the units where Pathways students were housed. Some officers even came to the prison on their days off to attend school events. If custody staff members were not convinced of the program's merits, they could make it difficult for instructors to enter and move around the facility, which caused the instructors to be late for class or miss class altogether. Custody staff also may not call down the students for class. Their support also was important when classes occurred at night or on weekends, when facilities typically have a smaller number of staff members working.

The facility-based education staff also may affect how Pathways is implemented. They must create rosters and call-out lists, coordinate class schedules and classroom space, collect and report program data, and address student concerns. It is important to get them on board as well, from the principal to the counselor, because the time commitment required of them is high.

Pathways College Administrators and Instructors

The North Carolina Pathways instructors typically coordinated their work through a college administrator and the facility-based education coordinator. Although many of the college instructors working with the Pathways student population viewed doing so as rewarding, the students did present challenges. For example, according to one college administrator, instructors suspected that some students struggled with attention-deficit/hyperactivity disorder (ADHD) or other learning disabilities and needed to make adjustments to accommodate those challenges.

For many college instructors, teaching within a correctional environment was a new experience, and some found the security requirements, procedures for getting approval to bring in course materials or videos, and the importance of meeting key deadlines in a controlled movement environment onerous or confusing. Instructors also needed to allot enough time to enter the facility and pass through the security screenings. Although the instructors were given training, they still made mistakes in terms of knowing what they could and could not bring into a prison and what classroom materials were appropriate for prison-based students. This, in turn, added to the workload of correctional education staff, who had to develop the schedules in advance, arrange for inmates to be called out to attend classes, and approve all materials being brought into the facilities. Being well-prepared for class was critical, because once they were in the correctional facility, instructors could not go on the internet to look something up or print additional copies for students. The need to set clear expectations, define responsibilities for those involved in making Pathways work, and take into account the burden the program may place on facility staff was a key lesson learned.

Release Process

From the perspective of the Pathways navigators and other LRC staff, it was helpful to attend the prerelease success team meetings to meet the Pathways students and to help develop transition plans for them. It also enabled them to answer the questions the students had. With only three release communities and a handful of Pathways-designated facilities, the success teams in some cases had to travel far to meet with the students, and this, in turn, meant fewer visits.

The Pathways navigators and LRC staff observed that the students expressed several concerns about release, particularly around finding housing and employment and reuniting with their families. Some students had few resources or little family support; for them, it was particularly important to assess their needs and link them to services in preparation for returning to the community. As we discuss in Chapter Three, the success teams helped provide some reassurance to students that they would be supported as they navigated these various challenges.

Because students were required to transfer to one of six prison facilities that housed the Pathways Program in North Carolina, students in some cases were moved to a facility far from their families. This made it difficult for some family members to visit the student while he or she was incarcerated and, as discussed in Chapter Three, presented a difficult decision for some students as to whether to return to one of the three release communities if it meant being far away from their families.

Finally, the relatively small number of students who had completed a college application, were accepted to a college, or had submitted a financial aid application while incarcerated meant that these activities largely had to occur after release to the community. This suggests that perhaps this process could have been done earlier while the Pathways participants were still in prison.

CHAPTER THREE

The North Carolina Pathways Program's Community and Reentry Component

As described earlier in this report, site visits were conducted in each of the three designated release communities to document the experiences the Pathways students had with reentry and with continuing their education programs postrelease. Information was gathered from students, LRC staff, college faculty and administrators, PPOs, and transitional housing managers about the factors that supported or hindered the students' success. We learned that many students remained in the Pathways Program despite facing a variety of reentry challenges. These students, as well as those who had to leave the program for family and other reasons, reported feeling grateful for the educational opportunities provided by Pathways. Many said that the program gave them meaning and purpose while incarcerated and a better chance to succeed postrelease.

In the following sections, we summarize the site visit findings based on the interviews and focus group discussions and include an overview of the community and reentry component, challenges with implementation, and the adjustments made to the program. In this chapter, we also include a discussion of the findings and lessons learned and a summary of the students' and staff members' assessments of the program.

The Community Component

The three release communities—Greenville/Pitt County, Charlotte/Mecklenburg County, and Asheville/Buncombe County—were selected because they had existing organizations that could serve as LRCs and provide the reentry services planned for the Pathways students. In Greenville, such services came from Life of NC/Strive NC. In Charlotte, they came from the Mecklenburg County Re-Entry Services, and in Asheville, they came the Buncombe County Reentry Council.

At the same time, NCDPS recognized that it needed to give these organizations additional resources to strengthen their capacity and support the Pathways work. Each community, therefore, received the same amount of funding to tailor reentry services to the students who chose to be released into their communities. In addition to the general services provided to all of their reentry clients (e.g., job referrals, housing assistance, bus cards, counseling, program referrals), the LRCs provided Pathways students with laptops, rental assistance, and tuition reimbursement for those who did not qualify for federal student aid. The LRCs also received funding to hire a Pathways navigator to serve as a liaison between the students and the local community colleges, which were AB-Tech in Asheville, Pitt Community College in Greenville, and CPCC in Charlotte. Another critical feature of the Pathways community component was that NCDPS asked its community corrections district supervisors to assign the students to PPOs who were supportive of the Pathways Program.

As we summarize in Table 3.1, of the 165 Pathways students released from prison, 29 were released to Greenville/Pitt County, 54 were released to Charlotte/Mecklenburg County, and 53 were released to Asheville/Buncombe County. Twenty-nine students dropped out of the program after release.

As of August 2018, 145 students had exited the postrelease component of the Pathways Program. As indicted in Table 3.2, 68 students exited voluntarily and 31 students were involuntarily removed. Of those who exited, 11 earned a postsecondary credential and 35 had completed the postrelease component of the Pathways Program.

When we look across all the students who participated in the community component of the Pathways Program, Table 3.3 shows that 1,552 credits were earned. The total number of credentials earned was 15, including eight AAS degrees, five Associate in Arts degrees, and two certificates.

Table 3.1
Number of Pathways Students Participating in the Community Component of the Program, by Release Community, as of August 2018

Release Community	LRC	Community College	Total Number of Pathways Students Released from Prison to Each Location
Greenville/Pitt County	Life of NC/Strive NC	Pitt Community College	29
Charlotte/Mecklenburg County	Mecklenburg County Re-Entry Services	CPCC	54
Asheville/Buncombe County	Buncombe County Reentry Council	AB-Tech Community College	53
Released to other counties	N/A	N/A	29
Total released	N/A	N/A	165

SOURCE: Data were provided by NCDPS.

NOTE: N/A = not applicable.

Table 3.2
Number Exiting the Postrelease Component of the North Carolina Pathways Program, as of August 2018

Statistic	Number
Total number that exited the postrelease component of the program	145
Voluntarily exited program	68
Involuntarily removed from the program	31
Exited the program credentialed	11
Completed the postrelease component of the program	35

SOURCE: Data were provided by NCDPS.

Table 3.3
Postrelease Statistics for the North Carolina Pathways Program, as of August 2018

Statistic	Number
Total credits earned postrelease	1,552
Total credentials earned postrelease	15
• Certificates earned	2
• Associate in Arts degrees	5
• AAS degrees	8

SOURCE: Data were provided by NCDPS.

Implementation Challenges and Adjustments Made

Overall Challenges

As is true for most returning citizens, reentry was a very challenging time for the Pathways students. Within a few weeks of being released, the students were expected to enroll in college full-time; secure part-time employment; find suitable housing arrangements; address transportation needs; reunite with family members; and, in some cases, resume parental and financial responsibilities for their families while managing and seeking treatment for any substance abuse, depression, anxiety, or other mental health issues. As one community college administrator noted, Pathways students were a microcosm of the range of issues that affect most community college students; the difference was that Pathways students had to address all these common challenges within a short time frame while they were assimilating to life outside of prison. He described their situation as follows: "Unlike the general population, the Pathways students are experiencing all of the problems all at once. They face immediate challenges with housing, jobs, family, lack of [a] support network . . . . [I]t's like the Pathway[s] students' treatment plan is a nuclear reactor versus a chemo plan dosed out over a year." A Pathways navigator further observed that many of the students who were not from that area struggled with being away from family and being unfamiliar with the local community.

Pathways students were referred to a range of services by the Pathways Program. In Table 3.4, we summarize the type and number of referrals made over the course of the program. Housing, employment, and transportation were among the top needs of Pathways students, as indicated by the number of referrals for each of these services. Referrals to family services were also common. Referrals for substance abuse services were more than twice as common as for mental health services. One PPO said that mental health issues were common among Pathways students and her other clients. She reported that "many of them struggle with mental health issues like anxiety, bipolar [disorder], and schizophrenia. Many of these have been flagged based on the risk assessment." The PPO also reported substance abuse as a challenge and that regular drug tests are a requirement for most transitional houses.

Funding Challenges and Adjustments

To help address reentry challenges, NCDPS used Pathways funding to establish or expand the services provided by LRCs in the three release communities. Pathways funding specifically was used to fund services (e.g., reentry assistance and tuition assistance) and for a Pathways navigator in each of the release communities. The majority of the Pathways students said that they would not have been able to stay committed to the program if it was not for the support they received from the LRCs. Such support included assistance with housing, bus passes or money for gas, employment, food, supplies for classes and their jobs (e.g., equipment, uniforms, and books), childcare, doctor visits, drug treatment, and counseling.

Although each release community received the same budget from the Pathways initiative, the funding was spent differently depending on the size and needs of the student population and available community resources. The type of organization that

Table 3.4
Referrals to Services in the Community, as of August 2018

Type of Service	Total Number of Referrals
Housing	148
Employment	145
Transportation	143
Family services	141
Substance abuse	135
Mental health	57
Financial	23
Other	193

SOURCE: Data were provided by NCDPS.

NOTE: An individual student could receive more than one referral.

served as the LRC also affected how funding was spent. For example, the Asheville LRC was a nonprofit and a county contractor; as a result, it had access to government administrative supports and the benefits afforded to nonprofits (e.g., half-price bus passes). The Charlotte LRC, however, was part of the county government and had access to government supports, but also had to comply with government rules and regulations (e.g., it was prohibited from issuing gift cards to students). The Greenville LRC was a nonprofit that had a history of providing reentry services to the community (e.g., food pantry and donated clothing) and was able to leverage many of these services to support its Pathways work.

The students noticed these differences among the LRCs and release communities and shared this information with one another. For example, one of the three communities gained a reputation—justly or unjustly—among the incarcerated Pathways students as having better housing, more-progressive community members and employers, and greater services and supports available. Additionally, the community college in that release community had only one main campus, which made it easier for the LRC staff to meet with students and for students to provide peer support to one another. For these and other reasons, more Pathways students chose to be released to that community than was originally projected. As a result, that LRC began to run out of funds in the last year of the project and students in this release community were forced to pay for a greater portion of their rent or for all of their rent earlier than expected. Although the other release communities may not have been perceived by the Pathways students as having as many services and supports, the other LRCs were able to maintain the same level of financial support to the students in their communities through the end of the initiative.

Even within the same community, students were sensitive to differences in support provided by the LRCs to the Pathways participants. For example, the Pathways Program paid the tuition for students who did not qualify for federal student aid because of past loan defaults. Some of the students who did qualify for federal student aid reported feeling that they deserved some other type of support from the Pathways Program that equaled the amount of tuition that Pathways did not have to cover for them. Students also reported feeling that those who were released from prison earlier in the four-year pilot received more rental support and other services than those who were released closer to the end of the pilot. In their view, Pathways funding should have been spread more equally across the students. However, NCDPS intentionally gave the LRCs authority to tailor their support to the students' needs rather than provide each student with the same level of support. However, this led to the unintended consequence that students were suspicious of how the Pathways funding was being spent. As described by one LRC administrator, "While the LRC staff respect that every client is different, inconsistency with incentives has created more challenges and tension between students and LRC staff. Also, students try to go around LRC staff and ask for exceptions from Raleigh [the state DPS office], which also can hurt trust."

Housing, Employment, and Transportation Challenges and Adjustments

Housing, employment, and transportation presented other implementation challenges. Even before they were released, Pathways students were concerned about housing. Many were worried about being placed in a transitional house in a bad neighborhood or with troubled formerly incarcerated individuals. Although some of the Pathways students were satisfied with their transitional houses, several of them were placed in houses that added stress to their lives. Issues students cited included bedbugs, lack of heat or air conditioning, no WiFi, roommates with addiction or mental health issues, or long commutes to the college campus. Some students also reported feeling that the cost of the rent was too high given the quality of the housing and having to share bedrooms. Conversely, the LRC staff noted that some of the students who were able to rent their own apartments, typically through financial support from their families, struggled without the structure provided by a transitional house; such structure included having a house manager, a signed agreement, curfew, and random drug testing.

In one of the release communities, the housing manager was well respected by the students. He would help them with transportation issues and encourage them to stay in the program. However, that was not the case in all the release communities. Many students, as a result, wanted to make enough money so that they could move out of transitional housing and get their own apartments.

Finding employment was a top priority for most students, with most finding temporary employment within a few weeks of release. As one student noted, "I got a job three days before I got out. Not the best job. While I was working, I applied for some other jobs, but a background check killed it instantly. Now [I am] doing [college] work study." Other Pathways students relied on their LRCs for support, but the level of support varied by release community. In one release community, for example, the Pathways navigator was able to refer students almost immediately to temporary job positions after release. She used a temporary agency that placed students with employers that did not require background checks. Other students struggled to find employment. One student with a history of substance abuse said that his PPO stopped him from getting a warehouse stocking job because it included stocking alcohol. Another student said that his class schedule made it difficult to find a well-paying job.

Finding the right balance between work and attending college also was a challenge. Many of the students said that they felt pressure to work more than part-time, with some working for as many as 80 hours while attending school full-time. Others reported dropping out of the Pathways Program because they could not balance a full-time job with school. As one student admitted, "I was supposed to enroll [in college courses] for the summer, but I have mandatory overtime for my job. And I had been asking for overtime because I knew time was becoming short for the funding of the program, so I didn't want to be stuck without a plan."

In addition, in all three release communities, public transportation was not reliable or efficient. For example, Asheville is a rural community with a less extensive bus system than Charlotte. Furthermore, the Asheville bus system did not run late into the evening. This made it challenging for some students to get from their college courses to jobs and for some to return to their housing units by the PPO curfew. In Charlotte, the community college had five campuses that were widely spread out, thus making it challenging for some students to get to their classes. Also, although the LRCs provided bus passes, some of the students commented that they had to travel to the LRC to get a bus pass. These transportation problems only compounded the scheduling issues the students faced in balancing work and school. Many of the students, therefore, worked additional hours so that they could purchase their own cars.

Lessons Learned

The implementation of the community and reentry component of the Pathways Program, including the challenges and adjustments described earlier, resulted in several important lessons learned for North Carolina. Most notably, the students were greatly affected by a range of individuals in their lives, from staff affiliated with the Pathways Program to family members. The following sections describe these lessons learned and the students' and staff members' assessments of the program.

Guidance Received from a Trusted Person of Authority

Across all three communities, the Pathways students often cited the benefits they received from having a trusted person of authority to provide critical guidance, support, and encouragement throughout the reentry process and the community portion of the Pathways Program. The person of authority in the community most commonly cited by the students varied, but typically that person was the student's Pathways navigator, PPO, or community college instructor. This was particularly true for students whose families were not nearby or able to provide a positive support network.

For many students, the Pathways navigator was instrumental in facilitating college enrollment and linking students to college services (e.g., tutoring and the federally funded Student Support Services), employment opportunities, and reentry supports. However, the level of support provided by the different navigators—there was one per release community—varied. One navigator was described as very hands-on, holding office hours at the community college and sending encouraging texts to the students. For other students, their navigator was less proactive, and they instead turned to other persons of authority, family members, and students for advice and help. As one student commented, "I didn't have the supportive cast [from the LRC and navigator] I thought I had been promised when I got out." Instead, his family and PPO ended up playing those roles.

As was the case with that student, PPOs were cited by some of the Pathways students as important parts of their support systems. This was facilitated by NCDPS

Community Corrections hand-picking PPOs who were receptive to the Pathways Program to be assigned to the students. For example, in one reentry community, the PPO was selected to work with Pathways students because of his background in social work. He helped to fill in the gaps not addressed by the Pathways navigator, who did not connect as well with the students. Students reported that this PPO encouraged them to remain in the program and helped them solve issues that were hindering their persistence. That same PPO, though, noted that it was not appropriate for him to interact with the students at the college, because it could inadvertently stigmatize the students. He believed that that role was better suited for the Pathways navigator.

In another community, students reported having a PPO who was unfamiliar with the program and who felt that his primary job was to strictly enforce the conditions of parole. In this case, the PPO was perceived as being unsympathetic to transportation limitations that made it challenging for students to get to work and school within the curfew. Students also reported that some of their PPOs did not allow them to leave the county to see their families or have family members stay with them when visiting. This created additional emotional and financial stress for those students.

All of the students said that their college instructors treated them the same as they treated other college students. The instructors we interviewed also expressed their commitment to the Pathways Program and students. One instructor spent additional time encouraging his students, providing flexibility in scheduling their required lab work, and helping them connect to employers. Many of the students also reported that they benefited from the various support staff and services at the community colleges, including the financial aid office; admissions office; Student Support Services (a federal TRiO program designed to provide services to individuals from disadvantaged backgrounds); and writing, tutoring, and advising centers. In one release community, an administrative assistant in the college counseling office became the de facto liaison for the Pathways Program and a mentor for the students. He also had been incarcerated and, therefore, was able to model for the students how to move past their incarceration and earn a college degree. In his view, this shared history with the students was very important because "there's going to come a point of time where they have to get something off their chest that they can't tell a PO [probation officer]—they need to tell someone who understands what they are going through."

Regardless of who the trusted person of authority was for the students, most of these individuals indicated that more communication with the Pathways Program state staff and LRC staff was needed. Because the Pathways navigators, PPOs, and college instructors were on the front lines and interacted most with the students, it was important that they had a solid understanding of the program to avoid misinformation. For example, to help facilitate this communication, a PPO in one of the release communities attended LRC staff meetings once per month. These meetings gave him the opportunity to learn more about the program and the students and share what he was seeing in the field.

The Pathways navigators, PPOs, and instructors also pointed out that many of the students were reluctant to ask for help. As one navigator described,

> Some of the participants wait until the last minute to come and talk about school or talk about a class. The response we get all the time is, "I'm trying to make sure I was doing my piece, so I've got to handle this because I'm a grown man." Yeah, you're grown, but you still need assistance. . . . You're not going to be perfect—you have to ASK for help but also, we guide you; we don't tell you what to do.

According to this navigator, asking for help was more challenging for the male participants than the female participants, but with both genders, venting their frustrations to someone they trusted was needed "[b]ecause until they empty out, they can't hear anyway. So, let them empty out their fears of what they think is going to happen. After that, help them get clarity on where they want to be."

Support and Pressure from Families

Another important component of some students' support system was family members. As one PPO commented, families can be part of the "restoring process." Students reported that their families provide them with motivation to stay in the program and help with housing, transportation, clothing, childcare, and food. Yet for many students to remain in the program, they had to agree to be released to a community that was not near their families or children. Although they knew that their education would help their families in the long run, it was a very difficult choice to make. They reported feeling homesick and having trouble visiting their families because of parole restrictions and time constraints.

For other students, choosing to be released to a community far from their families was intentional—they needed a clean break. Having some distance from their hometowns enabled them to get away from bad influences and to start anew. Some students reported that the distance helped to alleviate pressure to begin providing financial and emotional support to their family and children immediately.

Regardless of proximity, many students still felt compelled to support their families. The types of support varied but included taking care of elderly or sick parents and grandparents, contributing financially (e.g., either directly or through child support), and resuming parental responsibilities for their children. Several of the mothers in the program, for example, shared that they felt guilty for being absent from their children's lives while incarcerated and, as a result, wanted to take over all parental responsibilities as soon as they were released. As one student said, "I missed five years of my daughter's life, I don't want to miss any more." Balancing school, work, and their children, though, took its toll on the mothers. One student admitted that she felt like she was failing as a mother. Another student commented that "[b]alancing all my responsibilities is hard. Something has to give. I feel very overwhelmed."

Students' Overall Assessments of the Program

Regardless of the challenges and obstacles the students faced in continuing the Pathways Program after release, they were very grateful for the opportunity to earn a PSE credential. Although they were limited to a terminal AAS degree while incarcerated, the students were pursuing a variety of educational opportunities in the community. They were able to enroll in programs that led to higher-level degrees or had different focus areas than the few majors that were provided in the prison portion of the program.

For future programs like Pathways, the students recommended providing more academic and career counseling and a greater selection of PSE programs in prison. This, in turn, would allow incarcerated students to enroll in prison-based programs that align with their career interests and would guarantee that more credits earned in prison would apply to PSE programs postrelease.

Furthermore, the students reported believing that the few Pathways participants who were permitted to participate in the study release program while incarcerated had access to a wider variety of PSE offerings and were better prepared for the transition into the community. They therefore recommended that future programs provide more study release options.

The Pathways students also thought that the selection process for the Pathways Program could have been more stringent to ensure that participating individuals had the education and motivation levels needed to be successful in both the prison and community components. As one student noted, "There were a lot of guys who didn't have any business to be in the program and were a distraction. [The program] wasted resources on them."

Pathways students also recommended better communication from Pathways staff and fewer "incentives" or "handouts" (e.g., promising to pay rent for a set number of months) to participate in the program. A student described the problem as follows:

> [Communication was a problem] from initial recruitment and the dream we were sold. The reality doesn't meet what we were told. Originally [we were told that Pathways] was a two-year program and then [it] moved to a year. Some of us have only been out for a few months and will be responsible for our own bills. But this isn't fair since some students aren't getting the same support. I don't want to sound entitled and ungrateful, because they gave me an opportunity to not go home and move forward with my future. The end of the support is very abrupt. We were only to work part-time hours and dedicate ourselves to school. But now we are expected to pay full-time bills with part-time jobs.

Many students agreed that the incentives initially promised were more of a distraction—particularly when they did not come to fruition—than a help. Rather, the students recommended focusing on the unique education opportunities provided by the program. As one student noted, "[Pathways] is a good program regardless. They should have been more factual [and] realistic with what could be offered." Although the Pathways students indicated that the incentives were not needed to encourage students to enroll in the program, they admitted to struggling with balancing competing responsibilities and demands on their time and were appreciative of the financial assistance and other support they received from the LRCs.

Some students tried to address their scheduling issues by enrolling in online courses at the community colleges. However, one student admitted that it was challenging to commit the time needed to be successful in an online course when other demands, like a job, were competing for his time. He described the challenge as follows:

> To me it is the online classes is what work affected the most. Because when you are in class you are there. But when you have [to] go to work—it is the online classes that will suffer when you get too many work hours because it is your responsibility to do the classes on your own time. So, it gets down to—am I going to sleep or am I going to do the online class. I don't think I could have done it if I had all in-person classes, so maybe there is some kind of balance where I can work X number of hours and still do the classes. Again, if I didn't have to pay for food and some stuff like that, it may have been different.

Several students also reported relying on their families for financial support and encouragement, and many students struggled with their decision to be released to a community far away from their families. They described feeling guilty and longing for the stability their families could provide. Pathways students, therefore, recommended that future programs provide more release community options so that the students are not forced to make the choice between their families and earning a postsecondary credential.

Despite these challenges, the maturity and motivation of many of the students were evident in the focus groups. Many students described how committed they were to turning their lives around and reported feeling that it was up to them to stay focused. College instructors and reentry staff also commented on the maturity and dedication of the students. One LRC director pointed out that the students were earning high grades and that many had been placed on the community college president's list for good academic standing.

The students also indicated that they wanted to make sure that the Pathways Program, or something similar, would be made available to other incarcerated students. If that happened, they had the following advice for other incarcerated individuals considering enrolling in such a program:

- "You have to be focused and patient."
- "Venture outside your comfort zone and make connections."
- "Be honest with yourself as to what you can/cannot do with a felony record."
- "You have got to meet the program halfway—put your best foot forward."

- "Take it one day at a time. There is a lot that's going to happen, but don't rush it. Take your time."
- "Don't be afraid to ask for help and ask questions."
- "Take advantage of it, take it seriously—if you don't take it seriously, let someone else have that opportunity."

Local and State Staff Members' Assessments of the Program

Staff at the local and state levels also were grateful for the Pathways Program because it gave them additional resources to support reentry, strengthened the capacity of the LRCs, and built support for education to be part of the state's reentry approach. Like the students, they had recommendations for future programs like Pathways.

First, they recommended providing more LRC staff time. The LRC staff in the three release communities agreed that the Pathways students took most of their time. One LRC staff member described this challenge as follows:

> Unlike other clients, the Pathway[s] students are with you for two years. They also have more challenges because they are trying to balance full-time school and work, whereas the other clients are normally not doing both. Also, many of the Pathways students aren't from the community, which creates other transition challenges like being away from family, not knowing how the public transit system works, [and] housing.

The local and state staff members also recognized the challenges with communication and recommended that future programs be clearer and more consistent about requirements and benefits. As one LRC staff member noted, "If you are not clear and you speak in generic terms, people hear what they already have been thinking—like, you may say I'm going to help you with housing and they may hear you are going to get me an apartment. So, we had a period of time when we had to bring clarity to it."

With regard to the in-prison component, the staff recommended a longer pilot to provide the colleges with more time to work out the "kinks" and the students with more time to earn a postsecondary credential prior to release. They also thought that a longer pilot would have motivated more incarcerated individuals to earn their high school equivalency so that they too could enroll in the Pathways Program. In addition, a community college administrator suggested creating a statewide plan for the in-prison education component to eliminate duplication among participating colleges and provide more transfer options for students after their release. He and other staff agreed that many of the Pathways students struggled with being far away from home. Despite being "blown away" by how the students were doing, he said that several students dropped out of the program to be with their families.

Similar to the Pathways students, the staff thought that the program needed a stronger student selection process and more college and career counseling. They noted that the students' skills in the first year were weaker than expected, which forced the college staff to reevaluate the courses being offered. Many students were enrolled in programs that did not align with their career interests. Several staff members suggested providing students with more academic and career counseling to ensure that students' career goals were realistic and aligned with the program. Otherwise, as pointed out by a college staff member, the students will turn to each other for advice, which is good in many respects but can steer them in the wrong direction when it comes to academics and career advice. He also said that changing majors after release created articulation problems for the students. Not all the courses offered in prison applied to their programs postrelease. Also, some students were forced to retake their college placement tests. He recommended providing students with a portfolio that includes their transcripts, test scores, and other information needed to facilitate college reenrollment in the community.

Staff members also agreed with students that the program's incentives were more of a distraction than a help. For example, as noted earlier, inconsistency in the incentives provided led to misunderstandings and tension between the students and LRC staff. Also, students tried to go around LRC staff and ask for exceptions from the state office, which further strained the relationship between the LRC staff and students. An LRC staff member described the situation as follows:

> I learned [to] be consistent and even across the board—whatever you do for one, they will communicate and then you have to do it for the other Pathway[s] students. I was getting pushback from Raleigh saying everyone is different, the support you give should be case by case—I understand that in theory, but the truth is if this student says he has a problem and needs help with X, then you [have] 20 other students with the same problem. I'm down here on the ground and so I know what is happening.

One approach that was consistent across the three LRCs was the Pathways navigator position. Everyone agreed that the navigator was critical to the success of the program, but they had recommendations for how the position could be strengthened. One college administrator recommended embedding the Pathways navigator role at the college or having the navigator be a shared position between the LRC and college. Similarly, a navigator noted the importance of having a workspace at the college and regular office hours. Several LRC staff members pointed out that the navigator position required more than the ten hours per week allocated by the Pathways Program.

By and large, the state and local staff members we interviewed said that most of the challenges they experienced with the Pathways Program came from the fact that they "were building the plane as we were flying it."

Discussion

Many of the challenges Pathways students reported as part of their transition to the community are common to the reentry process in general (Visher and Travis, 2003). Reentry is a challenging time for most individuals and can be overwhelming for many. Most states release individuals from prison with typically $20 to $100 in gate money, a bus ticket to an in-state location, a single set of clothes, and prescription medicine that may last them from between one week to several months (Jonson and Cullen, 2015). For individuals returning to local communities, the most-significant barriers to successful reentry include difficulties in finding housing and employment, reuniting with family and children, and obtaining health care to address substance abuse or mental health treatment needs (Travis, 2005). In addition, such individuals must meet basic needs, such as obtaining food, clothing, and transportation. Pathways students were no different in the types of needs they had; the top four referrals to services were for housing, employment, family reunification, and substance abuse treatment services.

Research has shown the importance of conducting detailed needs assessments before release and developing reentry plans tailored to an individual's needs and situation (Petersilia, 2003). The creators of the Pathways Program understood the importance of conducting such assessments. By structuring the success teams to engage the key players in working with the individual student to develop a transition plan prior to their release, Pathways administrators tried to ensure that a robust reentry plan was in place that was tailored to the needs of the individual students and that services were available in the local communities to which they would return.

Much of the failure that returning citizens experience occurs in the first six months to a year after their release, with more than two in five people (just under 45 percent) arrested by the end of their first year (Jonson and Cullen, 2015). Furthermore, two-thirds will be rearrested within three years (Langan and Levin, 2002; Durose, Cooper, and Snyder, 2014). Research has shown that returning citizens are particularly vulnerable in the first few weeks of release from prison, with peak rates for recidivism occurring in the days and weeks immediately following release (National Research Council, 2008).[1] The creators of the Pathways model recognized the importance of connecting students with Pathways navigators (even prior to release from prison) who could link them to reentry support services and facilitate their enrollment in local community colleges right away. The Pathways navigators were seen as a key source of support and a problem-solving resource for students as they transitioned back to the community. Furthermore, Pathways used part of its funding to build up the reentry infrastructure

---

[1] A retrospective cohort study by Binswanger et al. (2007) highlighted that those released from prison have substantial health risks and higher mortality rates than the general population. A key finding was that inmates released from prison had a high risk of death, particularly during the first two weeks following release, with the leading causes of death being drug overdose, cardiovascular disease, homicide, and suicide.

in the three release communities to ensure that the services needed by students would be available.

In addition, as a key component of the program, Pathways students were to be assigned to PPOs who were specially selected because of their knowledge and support of the program's goals and of education in general. Although not all students ended up with such a PPO, the Pathways students who did commented that having such a PPO was a key source of support for them out in the community. Research has shown the importance of the client–parole officer relationship. For example, Blasko et al.'s (2015) study of parolees randomized to a collaborative intervention versus traditional supervision found that parolees assigned to the collaborative intervention endorsed higher relationship ratings of increased caring, fairness, and trust to their parole officers than those who were assigned to traditional supervision. Higher relationship ratings were also associated with a lower violation rate. The authors concluded that when parolees perceived their relationships with their parole officers as positive, they were more likely to achieve better outcomes. Kennealy et al. (2012) similarly found that parolee–parole officer relationships characterized by a firm, fair, and caring approach helped protect against rearrest among general offenders. In a study of 109 parolees without mental illness, the authors found that firm, fair, and caring relationships helped protect against rearrest among general offenders even after accounting for offenders' preexisting personality traits and risk for recidivism.

Finally, research has long recognized the important role of family in successful reentry. Like the Pathways students, many individuals depend on family members or other relatives or friends for financial, housing, and emotional support upon release from prison. Research has shown that greater contact with family during incarceration is associated with lower recidivism rates (Adams and Fischer, 1976; Hairston, 2002). Prisoners with close family ties have lower recidivism rates than those without such attachments (La Vigne et al., 2004; Visher and Travis, 2003). Having said that, although families serve as support systems, they may also facilitate continued offending or substance abuse behavior; moreover, some family members may choose to no longer have contact with the returning offender (Visher and Travis, 2003). Pathways administrators recognized the role family can play and, as part of the in-prison component of the program, tried to balance the need to house Pathways students in one of six correctional facilities while trying to support their ability to maintain contact with their families if they desired. However, because Pathways students were released to one of only three release communities, some students were unable to be with their families and support systems, which contributed to some students deciding to leave the program to move closer to their families. For others, however, it was seen as a welcome chance to start anew.

CHAPTER FOUR

Conclusions and Recommendations

The North Carolina Pathways Program offers valuable insights into the successes and challenges of implementing a PSE program designed to begin with college coursework while individuals are still incarcerated and then facilitate their reenrollment and continuation in the community postrelease. In this chapter, we summarize our observations about the qualitative outcomes of the program, as well as key findings and lessons learned. We then discuss a set of recommendations for stakeholders in other states interested in implementing college programs to improve educational outcomes for those incarcerated in their states. We end with a discussion of how the Pathways Program has affected and continues to affect PSE in prison in North Carolina.

Qualitative Outcomes

Although our evaluation focused on implementation issues (with an outcomes analysis planned in the future), our assessment is informative about the qualitative, near-term outcomes of the North Carolina Pathways Program. This summary is based on our interviews with staff and Pathways students and our own observations and assessment. We note that it is missing the perspectives of family members.

Revisiting the logic model for North Carolina's Pathways Program presented in Figure 1.1 in Chapter One, the in-prison component of the program

- allowed students to continue their education while incarcerated, focusing on career paths that would lead to postsecondary certifications, diplomas, and/or AAS degrees (versus simply taking courses to bide time while in prison)
- enabled many individuals to stay focused on education and made having infractions while incarcerated less likely
- provided the students with a sense of purpose, direction, and confidence
- helped create a positive bond among cohorts
- enabled the correctional staff to see the importance of education as part of the rehabilitative process

- helped many Pathways participants begin to rebuild relationships with their families.

The community component of North Carolina's Pathways Program

- helped participants stay focused on educational attainment upon their return to local communities
- provided critical reentry supports to students that facilitated the continuation of their education
- provided reentry staff and PPOs with access to new resources not previously available to them to help students returning from prison
- demonstrated students' motivation and maturity to educational institutions and employers
- built up LRC capacity in the three release communities, which, in turn, benefited other formerly incarcerated individuals in those localities.

Findings and Key Lessons Learned

If one was going to design and implement a college program based on the two-years-inside/two-years-outside model, what went well and what might be done differently? The experiences of the North Carolina Pathways Program and lessons learned provide rich insights as to how to structure similar college programs and should be instructive for those who may wish to implement a similar program model in their own states.

Pathways Students Were Seen as Dedicated and Mature

For the most part, Pathways students were seen as dedicated to furthering their education. The Pathways students we interviewed talked about their motivation for participating in the program, with many seeing it as an important chance to further their education and turn their lives around. Overall, they were grateful for the opportunity to participate in the Pathways Program.

Program staff, instructors, corrections officials, college staff, and reentry staff indicated that they were impressed with the maturity of many of the students, how hardworking they were, and how committed many of them were to make the most of this opportunity. As some instructors commented, students both in prison and out in the community showed a level of maturity and dedication that many instructors said was above what they typically see in community college students.

For many of the participants, Pathways came at the right time. They had already been focused on the future by taking whatever class was available to them while incarcerated prior to applying to Pathways. When we asked them about their education experience prior to Pathways, many reported that they had earned several other occupational credentials while incarcerated. However, Pathways was different in that it allowed them to earn a postsecondary credential and continue their education postrelease with the support of the LRCs.

It Takes Time To Set Up These Programs

An overarching lesson learned about the Pathways Program is that it takes time to implement a prison-based and community-based program with multiple partners and with a population that has diverse needs. State and local staff reported wishing that more time had been available to plan for the in-prison and community components. As noted by one college administrator, "Just as we started to figure it out, our time was up."

The staff supporting the Pathways Program also reported wishing that they could have offered students more time to participate in the program and earn a credential prior to release. The amount of developmental coursework Pathways students needed was more extensive than originally anticipated, which further truncated the time allotted for the in-prison component. Furthermore, as explained by the NCDPS Pathways administrator and confirmed by the experiences shared by the students who participated in the focus groups, the Pathways students did not have as many pressures on the inside as they had on the outside; thus, they would have been in a better position to complete a PSE program while in prison. The students also pointed out that the amount of time the different cohorts were in the in-prison component of the Pathways Program varied from two years to less than one year, which meant that some students received only a year of support while incarcerated and even less support once released. In general, the staff and students felt that to have a real impact on the system, one needed a longer commitment (a minimum of five years) for these types of initiatives.

In 2017 research on PSE in prisons, RAND and RTI researchers learned a similar lesson: It often takes incarcerated students longer to earn credentials and complete college coursework while incarcerated than it would take if they were out in the community (e.g., because fewer courses are offered per semester). Given this lesson, it is worth considering how to structure in-prison college programs so that students can start a PSE program early enough in their sentence to earn a credential before leaving prison, with the option of continuing their education out in the community. This also underscores the need to think about college programs extending out into the community and how to help individuals make that transition upon release.

The staff and students also reported believing that the shortness of the in-prison component of the Pathways Program may have prevented the "home growing" effect desired as part of the demonstration project. That is, one intended outcome of the in-prison component was that the Pathways Program would motivate other individuals in prison who were not selected for Pathways to earn their GEDs and enroll in college while incarcerated and then hopefully to continue their education out in the community.

Having the Pathways Program Embedded in NCDPS Was an Asset

Despite the challenges with implementation, North Carolina benefited from having the support of senior state officials. As a condition of funding, Pathways required that the program have key agency and senior leadership commitment to the program. In addition, it was important to have a strong Pathways administrator and leader who had credibility among the various stakeholders involved in implementing the program.

These educational programs occur within a correctional setting; thus, having department of corrections senior leadership support, as well as a senior administrator who was effective within that organization (as was the case with the North Carolina Pathways Program), was key to solving problems, getting and maintaining support at all levels of the department, and understanding the concerns of both correctional and educational staff and how to address them. The Pathways administrator had credibility with senior corrections leadership and with superintendents and correctional staff and community colleges, which enabled her to effectively navigate problems as they arose and to obtain key buy-in.

The Student Selection Process Could Have Been Improved

Both staff members and students reported feeling that the student selection process could have been improved to ensure that those selected were committed and motivated to further their education and to ensure that the Pathways Program was aligned with their career interests. They reported feeling that the selection criteria needed to place a greater emphasis on finding students who were truly committed to earning a credential. Despite North Carolina's extensive screening processes, not all selected students assimilated well into the program in the first year, and a few left the program for personal reasons or misconduct. Student recruitment and selection are resource-intensive and time-intensive processes and adjustments had to be made (e.g., North Carolina relaxed its selection criteria to get a sufficient pool of individuals eligible to apply to the program).

Instructors and students reported feeling that those who were not committed were a distraction and were more likely to drop out, thus wasting a spot in the program and the resources dedicated to the initiative. Those who were motivated reported being very grateful for the opportunity and dedicated to making the most out of the opportunity.

Communication Takes Time and Is Critical to Program Success

Another critical lesson learned from both the in-prison and community components was the need for regular communication among staff and students. At various points, there were misunderstandings about what was promised to the students, the expectations of the program, and how the Pathways students would fit into the larger correctional environment. As a result, the NCDPS staff learned that more time needed to be invested in communication with different stakeholders, including prison administrators, college faculty, and LRC staff. LRC staff, in particular, were on the front lines and interacted most with the Pathways students. Given that, they needed a solid and current understanding of the program to avoid miscommunication. Students' expectations also needed to be managed; they needed to be informed about program changes right away and the reasons for those changes.

There Is a Need for Staff Training and Support

Similar to the communication challenge, teaching in a correctional environment was a new experience for many college instructors, and some found the security requirements, procedures for getting approval to bring in course materials or videos, and the importance of meeting key deadlines in a controlled movement environment onerous or confusing. This, in turn, added to the workloads of correctional educational staff members, who must develop the schedules in advance, arrange for inmates to be called out to attend classes, and approve all materials being brought into the facilities. A key lesson learned was the need to set clear expectations and define responsibilities for those involved in making Pathways work, as was the need for those involved to recognize the burden such a program places on facility staff.

It also was important to perform outreach and educate correctional facilities' staff (including superintendents, assistant superintendents, correctional officers, and facility-based education staff) on an ongoing basis to get them on board and to continually reinforce the program's goals and structure.

Incarcerated Students Need More Opportunities to Prepare for Release

Reentry is a stressful time for incarcerated individuals; therefore, Pathways staff and students recommended that programs like Pathways embed more opportunities into the in-prison component to familiarize students with their release communities, particularly for students releasing to communities far from their homes. For example, the incarcerated students who participated in the study release program seemed to have an easier time with their transitions. Similarly, some Pathways students were incarcerated in prisons that were being served by the same community college they enrolled in postrelease and reported having a smoother transition than those students who had to change to a different college upon release.

The Pathways students also expressed appreciation for meeting with success teams prior to release. These meetings gave them the opportunity to get to know the reentry staff and their PPO prior to release, ask questions, discuss housing options, and plan for reenrolling in college.

As noted in Chapter Two, many students had not completed college or financial aid applications prior to release, suggesting that this process should be started earlier in the timeline, while students are still incarcerated.

Having Only Three Release Communities Made Sense Resource-Wise, but There Were Trade-Offs

Allowing the students to be released to communities closer to home could have eased the reentry process. However, having three release communities made sense resource-wise and enabled NCDPS to build up the reentry infrastructure and reentry services needed for Pathways. It also enabled NCDPS to develop the community college relationships necessary to implement the community component of Pathways. In addition, at that time, there were only five LRCs in the state; three of the five communities with LRCs were selected by the North Carolina Pathways Program as release communities to ensure that participants had access to reentry support when they returned to the community.

Although six correctional facilities had Pathways students for the in-prison component of the program, there were only three release communities to which they could return. In retrospect, it might have been better to have given Pathways students more options about which communities they returned to. Although some students needed a clean break from their families and hometowns, many students needed emotional and financial support from their families, and the distance ended up creating more stress. Being closer to their families may have helped encourage some of them to stay in their education program, rather than feeling that they had to make a choice between continuing their education versus being closer to family.

As one college instructor put it, there are 58 community colleges in North Carolina. If Pathways students had been able to attend a community college closer to their homes, it may have helped them continue their education. He observed that of those Pathways students who ended up dropping out of their local community colleges and returning home, some of them may have stayed in the program upon release from prison if they were able to continue their courses at a community college closer to home.

Funding Distribution Needs to Be Transparent and Equitable

Program funding was inconsistent across the release communities and even among students within the same community; in addition, the funding amounts changed over time. This proved to be problematic for the implementers of the community component of the Pathways Program (e.g., program staff, reentry staff, headquarters staff). For Pathways students, this eroded their trust and introduced uncertainty about the level and type of support they would have upon release to the community. Anxiety about paying for housing was particularly acute toward the end of the Pathways Program.

It also had a negative effect on the different cohorts released to the community in that they were aware that the amount of funding support Pathways students received from the program varied by cohort. Although the goal of tailoring the funding to individual students' needs was understandable, doing so in practice created confusion among the students and reentry staff and suspicion that what was originally promised was not forthcoming.

In retrospect, variations in the funding amount provided to the release communities and to the different Pathways cohorts caused some trust and communication problems and created uncertainty among the reentry staff about what resources they had to work with. Furthermore, the reentry staff were on the front lines in communicating these changes to Pathways students, who were bewildered but also mistrusted what was being told to them.

The Pathways Program officially ended right as the DoE introduced its three-year experimental program—the Second Chance Pell Experimental Sites Initiative—to make Pell Grants available to incarcerated individuals who otherwise met Title IV eligibility requirements. Sixty-seven colleges and universities in 27 states were awarded a grant under the Pell Pilot Program. Although North Carolina colleges that participated in the Pathways Program applied for funding, they were not selected for the Pell experiment. As one North Carolina administrator put it, "not receiving the Second Chance Pell funding broke [his] heart." They felt that they had learned so much from Pathways and continuation with Pell funding would have been important. However, they also noted that the Pell application process got them to think more long term and that they were looking into moving students from correctional facilities to other facilities that may have been a better fit in terms of the programs in which those facilities specialized.

In North Carolina prior to 2011, the state had a tuition waiver program. Interviewees were concerned that with Pathways ending, it may be the end of the road for these types of programs for students. Interviewees felt that the best chance of having college programming continue in prison was by having the tuition waiver reinstated, identifying another funding source (e.g., Pell Grant inmate exclusion removed), or obtaining state-level support.

Reentry Supports Are Critical to Students Being Able to Stay in Educational Programs

There are numerous reentry stressors that can affect students' decisions about whether to complete their education program out in the community, work full-time, or return home or move closer to family. Housing, employment, and transportation were among the key reentry supports needed by most students, in addition to having a Pathways navigator or trusted person of authority who could help link students to reentry services and help them navigate applying for both college and financial aid and signing up and beginning to take classes. Although Pathways was designed to get a lot of that done in the prerelease phase, it appears that much of it had to occur when individuals were released into the community. This suggests that the initial six months after release is a critical time for students to make those connections to be successful in transitioning to educational programs out in the community.

Reentry resources are critical to those returning from prison. NCDPS made sure that Pathways funding was used to build local reentry capacity in the release communities. From the evaluation results, it was clear that this was critical to Pathways. It also benefited others returning from prison to those communities. The PPOs assigned to the Pathways Program noted that they wished they could have offered to provide all of their clients with the same level of support and resources that were provided to the Pathways students.

Having the Pathways Navigator and Trusted Persons of Authority Is Important

Most interviewees felt that the Pathways navigator role was essential and was an important source of support for many of the Pathways students. Both college and LRC staff members suggested that more could be done to embed the navigator at the college, with one interviewee suggesting that the navigator position would be strengthened if it was shared between the LRC and the community college. Many interviewees felt that the navigator needed to be a full-time position, given the critical linkage role he or she played with reentry services and community colleges. In addition, having a navigator facilitate students' linkages to the community college and reentry services was seen as helping prevent students from standing out as being formerly incarcerated.

Having a trusted person of authority was clearly critical to students' success, particularly in the initial transition back to communities. In addition to the importance of the navigator, this study showed the importance of recruiting and training PPOs who are supportive of education and understand the program to work with the Pathways students. The students were appreciative of PPOs who treated them with respect and understanding and encouraged them to earn their credential or degree. Also, the PPO was more likely to understand where flexibility was needed to accommodate the challenges the students faced in going to school full-time, working, and trying to reunite with family.

Family Plays a Key Role in Students' Decisions and Success

From the beginning, NCDPS recognized that family played a key role in influencing a student's decision about whether to apply to the program. Upon release, family could either play a positive supporting role or represent a stressor, given the pressures they may place on students, either encouraging them to continue their education or to focus on full-time employment and helping support the family.

Many of the students were dealing with some complex family dynamics. For example, female students discussed the pressures of trying to be a full-time mother to their children and the negative comments they had received from their families. Men similarly talked about missing their young children and wanting to be a father figure for their children, but they were torn between finishing their education or working full-time and moving away from the release community. For other students, family was negative in terms of encouraging them to return to a life of crime; thus, they saw being away from family as helping them to change their lives. For these reasons, family reunification services will be important to have in place to help individuals sort through these dynamics.

Structuring the Program to Allow Students to Change Their Educational Paths upon Release Was Important

NCDPS set up the in-prison component to allow students to earn general credits as a foundation for earning an AAS degree upon release. This was important for several reasons. First, North Carolina's restriction that students could earn only an AAS and the offer of only three career paths was limiting to students. Upon returning to the community, some students changed their focus to something they were really interested in. Second, it was important to structure the in-prison component this way because of the length of time it typically takes in a correctional setting for students to make progress on their college coursework and degree paths.

Although Pathways students were offered academic and career counseling, both the staff and students reported feeling that more was needed to ensure that students' career goals were realistic and aligned with the Pathways Program. One college staff member noted that the students often turned to each other for advice, which is good in many respects but can also steer them in the wrong direction when it comes to academic or career advice.

Furthermore, the AAS programs offered in prison were limited to three majors (business administration, computer IT, and entrepreneurship), which did not always align with students' career interests. As discussed earlier, some students changed majors upon release from prison. In addition, there was recognition that it would have been helpful to allow students to earn certificates while incarcerated so that they would have those certificates when released.

Not all the credits transferred to the community college. For example, the success in study skills did not lead to any credits that a student could transfer upon release from prison. Because students went to different community colleges across the state, some had to retake their placement tests.

The Pathways Program Required Commitment and Sacrifices from All of the Stakeholders Involved

Students had to agree to be moved to the prison facilities where the program was being implemented and to be released to one of three communities that may be far away from their families. Students also had to agree to remain in medium-custody facilities to complete the in-prison component of the program. Facilities had to commit staff time to coordinate the program with other in-prison programming, allow students to live in separate housing units, and provide additional studying space. LRC staff had to dedicate the majority of their staff time to the Pathways students and develop or strengthen relationships with community colleges, transitional housing managers, and other community service providers. State administrations had to provide 25-percent match funding and staff time to plan, implement, and manage the program; agree to such policy changes as inmate transfers to Pathways-designated facilities; and place education holds to ensure that students stayed in designated facilities until they completed the program.

Recommendations for Other States on Implementing a Pathways-Like Model

The conclusions highlighted key lessons learned from North Carolina's experience in implementing a two-year-inside, two-year-outside PSE program model. In this section, we highlight the following key recommendations for policymakers in other states considering designing college programs for incarcerated adults:

- Structure the in-prison component of the college program to allow enough time for students to build general credit and earn certifications prior to release.
- Consider eliminating the state restriction on the types of postsecondary degree programs that can be offered in prison.
- Provide specific training to those staff members (e.g., custody, agency, reentry, and PPO staff) who will work with the students on an ongoing basis so that they understand the context and parameters of the program and can better support participants.
- Structure the program to allow students to initially attend college part-time in the community upon their release from prison. This would allow them to get acclimated and go through the reentry adjustment process. It also would relieve the stress of trying to go to college full-time while needing to work full-time.
- Include enough release communities in the program so students can live near their families and other supports.
- Invest in reentry infrastructure to ensure that robust reentry supports are available to students. Although colleges do not necessarily have to take on the role of being the reentry provider, there must be a mechanism to facilitate students' linkage to reentry services.
- Ensure that community colleges and other education providers are part of the reentry planning process and other processes to facilitate students' enrollment and reenrollment postrelease.
- Ensure that a navigator and other trusted persons of authority are in place. The Pathways navigator role was an essential source of support for many students and should be a full-time position. It is important that parole officers understand these programs and support individuals' participation in them.

- Have a dedicated, full-time program administrator for at least the first few years of program implementation. This individual would need to facilitate and build partnerships to support the in-prison and community components of the program. This individual also would need to be effective in addressing policy barriers.
- Ensure that long-term funding options are in place to sustain a college program once initial grant or foundation funding has ended.

How Pathways Has Affected Prison Programming in North Carolina

It is noteworthy that NCDPS continues to find ways to fund different components of Pathways after the demonstration project has ended. In addition, Pathways had an impact on how NCDPS now approaches higher education in prison and reentry planning.

As noted in Chapter One, prior to Pathways, individuals could take correspondence courses on their own, but there was no coordinated effort to provide a path toward a postsecondary degree or credential. Furthermore, there was no coordination around reentry. However, Pathways laid the groundwork for and showed what reentry planning should look like, including what the success teams should be doing, the importance of building relationships, and a focus on helping individuals develop a reentry plan to prepare them for release. As one NCDPS staff member observed, "There is also now a lot more coordination between prison and probation/parole officers and community resources as a result of Pathways." Furthermore, the NCDPS Pathways administrator noted that NCDPS is investing in training its staff to better equip them to have reentry conversations with individuals. Importantly, the NCDPS Pathways administrator emphasized that because of Pathways, education has become the fourth pillar of the department's reentry focus, which features housing, employment, and transportation as the other three pillars.

In addition, NCDPS has set up a PSE advisory committee as a result of Pathways that continues to discuss what they want prison education to entail in North Carolina. This has led to several colleges receiving grants (from a regional foundation) and has led the department to continue to do an inside and outside PSE program.

Finally, the NCDPS Pathways administrator noted that Pathways showed how important technology is in education and how it has served as a catalyst for change. As she noted, "postsecondary education cannot be complete if we don't look at the technology piece." One result of Pathways was the introduction of access to the internet, as discussed in Chapter Three. NCDPS's IT staff have developed their own intranet platform (called i-Net) to support PSE in prison and provide limited internet access. Furthermore, NCDPS continues to provide PSE classes in the facilities that featured the Pathways Program because the infrastructure is now in place to do so.

Overview of the Pathways Demonstration Project

The Pathways from Prison to Postsecondary Education demonstration project's model was grounded in research that demonstrated (1) the lack of education common to correctional populations and (2) the role that increased educational attainment plays in keeping formerly incarcerated people out of prison and in helping them become contributing members of families and communities (Vera Institute of Justice, 2012b). There was recognition that providing PSE in prison can be difficult for state corrections departments and continuing such efforts postrelease was rarely a priority. Furthermore, there was recognition that linking reentry with in-prison and community-based PSE was challenging to supervision agencies and reentry organizations.

The Pathways model featured the following key elements (Vera Institute of Justice, 2012b):

- Provide direct support for PSE in prison, including creating linkages between corrections departments and facilities and the community colleges in their states and regions.
- Build agreements between corrections departments and colleges regarding the eligibility of prison-based courses for degree credit and the transfer of those credits to community-based institutions of higher learning.
- Provide incarcerated students nearing release with guidance regarding continuation of their studies and pursuit of a degree or certification after release.
- Ensure that incarcerated students nearing release have opportunities for academic acceleration, needed documents, and a plan for their return to the community.
- Provide community-based counselors to assist formerly incarcerated students in transitioning to the community and in enrolling in institutions of higher education, especially community colleges.
- Assist formerly incarcerated students with tuition and provide other kinds of material support as needed.
- Provide mentoring, tutoring, and comprehensive supports and services to students once enrolled.
- Evaluate the progress of students academically, in employment and earnings, and in crime desistance.

- If success in these areas is demonstrated, build understanding and support for the importance of education of people in and after prison to public safety and strong families.

New Jersey was the first state invited to participate in the demonstration project, and six other states (Colorado, Michigan, New York, North Carolina, Oklahoma, and Washington) were subsequently invited to submit proposals. In addition to New Jersey, Michigan and North Carolina were selected in 2013 to participate in the Pathways demonstration project. Michigan and North Carolina received $1 million in incentive funding to pilot educational programming and reentry support services for adult offenders. New Jersey, which already had a PSE program called NJ-STEP, received $1 million to participate in the demonstration project. North Carolina and New Jersey were selected early in 2013, whereas Michigan's selection as a pilot state was not announced until May 2013, which gave Michigan somewhat less time to plan for implementing Pathways.

The incentive funding was designed to facilitate the repurposing and leveraging of existing revenue streams and encourage new public and private funds in support of the proposed efforts. To qualify for the funding, each state had to submit a detailed description of its project model and a plan for achieving its objectives. The Pathways project had two core requirements (Vera Institute of Justice, 2012b):

- States must provide an overall match of at least 25 percent, with 15 percent in the form of a cash match (from public and/or private sources) and 10 percent in-kind contributions to be distributed over the four years of the demonstration project.
- Each state must convene a leadership team, comprising public and private stakeholders, to oversee the development of the work and financing plans and sign the application affirming that they support the plans as presented. Members of the leadership team also must be willing to continue to provide oversight of the implementation, hold agencies and leaders to their commitments, and support the project's continuation and expansion if the pilots are successful.

In addition, to participate in the demonstration project, states were required to have the following specific commitments (Vera Institute of Justice, 2012b):

- commitment from the state executive and legislative leadership to support the pilot project with both policy and resources
- commitment from the department of corrections that all reasonable measures will be taken to minimize and mitigate these actions to ensure that educational programming could proceed as planned
- commitment from the director of the state parole or postrelease community supervision agency and a detailed plan from the head of the supervision agency for how the agency would align its practices to support the education effort

- commitment from and cooperation of local institutions of higher learning—whether a state college system or individual local community colleges or private universities—specifically, (1) certifying the credentials of corrections educators and the curricula used in corrections education programs for the purposes of granting credits to students for those courses after release; (2) signing articulation agreements with the corrections departments; (3) agreeing to provide tuition assistance to students when released; (4) offering academic counseling to incarcerated students before release; (5) offering courses taught by their staffs inside prisons; and (6) cooperating with mentoring and other support activities for previously incarcerated students on their campuses.

In addition, all stakeholders were asked to commit to cooperating with the evaluation of the Pathways Program.

The Cross-Site Logic Model

Figure A.1 provides an overview of the cross-site logic model and compares and contrasts similarities and differences in the three states' approaches to Pathways. For all three states, the inputs were similar in terms of resources and infrastructure and in states' expectations of the outcomes and impacts of the Pathways Program.

Where the states differed was in their approach and program features—that is, how each planned to achieve the desired outcomes and impacts. The in-prison implementation was core to the Pathways Program, and, as indicated in Figure A.1, although the states had similar elements for their educational activities and prerelease activities, they varied considerably in the types of educational and instructional supports and the supplemental services they planned to provide to Pathways students. In the following section, we compare and contrast the inputs of each Pathways Program across the three states for each of the four columns in Figure A.1.

Inputs

The inputs are the resources and infrastructure that were brought to bear to implement the Pathways demonstration project in each of the states. Table A.1 presents a summary of the inputs across the three states.

In terms of funding, as noted earlier, each of the states received $1 million in incentive funding to implement Pathways. Each state also was required to provide an overall match of at least 25 percent, with 15 percent in the form of a cash match (from public or private sources) and 10 percent in the form of in-kind contributions to be distributed over the four years of the project.

In-prison resources included department of corrections programming staff, correctional staff, educational staff, case management staff, and supervisory staff to facili-

Figure A.1
Cross-Site Logic Model

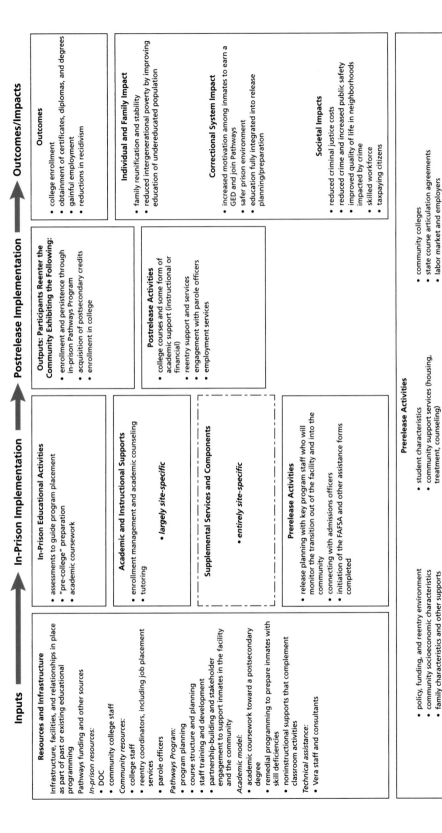

Inputs → In-Prison Implementation → Postrelease Implementation → Outcomes/Impacts

Resources and Infrastructure

Infrastructure, facilities, and relationships in place as part of past or existing educational programming
Pathways funding and other sources
In-prison resources:
- DOC
- community college staff
Community resources:
- college staff
- reentry coordinators, including job placement services
- parole officers
Pathways Program:
- program planning
- course structure and planning
- staff training and development
- partnership-building and stakeholder engagement to support inmates in the facility and the community
Academic model:
- academic coursework toward a postsecondary degree
- remedial programming to prepare inmates with skill deficiencies
- noninstructional supports that complement classroom activities
Technical assistance:
- Vera staff and consultants

In-Prison Educational Activities
- assessments to guide program placement
- "pre-college" preparation
- academic coursework

Academic and Instructional Supports
- enrollment management and academic counseling
- tutoring

   largely site-specific

Supplemental Services and Components

   entirely site-specific

Prerelease Activities
- release planning with key program staff who will monitor the transition out of the facility and into the community
- connecting with admissions officers
- initiation of the FAFSA and other assistance forms completed

Outputs: Participants Reenter the Community Exhibiting the Following:
- enrollment and persistence through in-prison Pathways Program
- acquisition of postsecondary credits
- enrollment in college

Postrelease Activities
- college courses and some form of academic support (instructional or financial)
- reentry support and services
- engagement with parole officers
- employment services

Outcomes
- college enrollment
- obtainment of certificates, diplomas, and degrees
- gainful employment
- reductions in recidivism

Individual and Family Impact
- family reunification and stability
- reduced intergenerational poverty by improving education of undereducated population

Correctional System Impact
- increased motivation among inmates to earn a GED and join Pathways
- safer prison environment
- education fully integrated into release planning/preparation

Societal Impacts
- reduced criminal justice costs
- reduced crime and increased public safety
- improved quality of life in neighborhoods impacted by crime
- skilled workforce
- taxpaying citizens

Prerelease Activities
- policy, funding, and reentry environment
- community socioeconomic characteristics
- family characteristics and other supports
- student characteristics
- community support services (housing, treatment, counseling)
- community colleges
- state course articulation agreements
- labor market and employers

NOTE: The dashed line indicates that the services and components are supplemental rather than required.

Table A.1
Inputs for the Pathways Demonstration Project

Michigan	North Carolina	New Jersey
	General Resources	
• preexisting infrastructure, facilities, and relationships • Pathways funding • DOC funding	• preexisting infrastructure, facilities, and relationships • Pathways funding • DOC funding • welfare funds	• Pathways funding • DOC funding • foundation funding • college funding
	In-Prison Resources	
• DOC staff (e.g., state-level education staff, principals, adult and vocational staff, employment counselors, unit managers, housing staff) • community college staff	• DOC staff (e.g., state and prison education staff, case managers, regional program coordinators, superintendents) • community college staff	• NJ-STEP staff (e.g., facility administrators, student advisory boards, supervisors of education, NJ-STEP institutional liaison, academic services, academic counselors) • community college and university staff (e.g., faculty site coordinators, faculty and instructors from colleges)
	In-Community Resources	
• community college staff • reentry councils and services • community corrections • labor ready (employment services) • other community resources	• community college staff • reentry council (e.g., reentry coordinators, job placement specialists, and Pathways navigators) • community corrections • other community resources (e.g., Joblink)	• two- and four-year college staff (e.g., consortium members, registrar and admissions officers, admissions counselors) • community corrections • halfway houses and housing coordinators (in future) • full-time Mountainview director • other community resources
	Pathways Program	
• program planning • course structure and planning • staff training • partnership-building and stakeholder engagement	• program planning • course structure and planning • staff training • partnership-building and stakeholder engagement	• consortium-building and stakeholder engagement • consortium director • program and overall continuum (inside to outside) planning • faculty, instructors, and staff training

Table A.1—Continued

Michigan	North Carolina	New Jersey
Academic Model That Supports:	**Academic Model That Supports:**	**Academic Model That Links Higher Education Infrastructure to Corrections**
• academic and occupational training • remedial education • assessment-driven placement • noninstructional supports • classroom instruction enhanced by computer technology • behavior management by students signing behavioral contract • multiple assessment opportunities	• academic and occupational training • remedial education • assessment-driven placement • noninstructional supports • classroom instruction enhanced by computer technology • behavior management by students signing behavioral contract	• degree-based coursework • remedial education • noninstructional supports
Technical Assistance		
• Vera staff and other consultants	• Vera staff and other consultants	• Vera staff and other consultants

tate the implementation of Pathways, as well as the classroom space, computer lab space, and housing arrangements needed to support these students. Depending on how each state's correctional system was organized, this could include PPOs or community supervision officers. In addition, the states varied in how much they offered Pathways students other services, such as drug counseling, or family reintegration workshops or programs.

Community resources included college staff who come into the prison to teach the Pathways students and college instructors at local community colleges or universities where Pathways students continue their education upon release. College administrative staff facilitated teaching in prison, the transfer of credits, and the enrollment of Pathways students in college courses upon release. Other community resources included reentry coordinators and reentry councils, job placement and employment services, college and employment counselors, and financial assistance.

Other inputs were the design of the Pathways Programs in each state, which included program planning, course structure and planning, and staff training and development. The academic model to be developed was intended to provide academic coursework that would lead to a postsecondary degree (A.A., A.S., AAS, B.A., or B.S.) and remedial programming or foundational courses to prepare students with math or reading skills deficits. Noninstructional supports included tutoring, study hall or study groups, and computer training. The states had leeway in designing their programs, particularly with respect to the academic and noninstructional supports to be provided and what supplementary services and prerelease activities would be offered to Pathways students.

Critical to Pathways' design, implementation, and success was the partnership-building and stakeholder engagement needed to support the program and inmates in the facility and as they move into the community.

In addition, Vera staff and consultants provided technical assistance to the three Pathways states during the demonstration project.

Consent Protocols and Focus Group Discussion Guide for Evaluation of the In-Prison Component of the Pathways Program

RAND Corporation

EVALUATION OF THE PATHWAYS FROM PRISON TO POST-SECONDARY EDUCATION PROGRAM

Consent Protocol for Administrators/Program Staff/Instructors

Project Leaders: Lois Davis (PI) and Robert Bozick (co-PI)
Tel. 310-393-0411
Email: lmdavis@rand.org; rbozick@rand.org

1. PURPOSE OF THE STUDY

The RAND Corporation, a non-profit research institution in Santa Monica, California, is conducting an evaluation of the Pathways from Prison to Post-Secondary Education Demonstration Project being led by the Vera Institute of Justice. The demonstration project is funded by five major foundations: the Ford Foundation, the Sunshine Lady Foundation, the Open Society Foundations, the W. K. Kellogg Foundation, and the Bill and Melinda Gates Foundation.

The Pathways demonstration project has provided selected states with incentive funding and technical assistance to expand access to higher education for people in prison and those recently released. The project seeks to determine whether access to postsecondary education, combined with supportive reentry services, can increase educational credentials, reduce recidivism, and increase employability and earnings. RAND was selected to conduct an independent evaluation of this demonstration project. This consent form pertains to the implementation study being conducted as part of the evaluation.

2. HOW WE SELECTED YOU

We are interviewing Pathways administrators, program staff, and instructors to understand the implementation of the Pathways demonstration project. We selected you because of your involvement with the Pathways pilot program within your state in one of these capacities.

3. WHAT WE WILL ASK YOU TO DO

For this evaluation study, we are interested in learning about Pathways program planning, program components, course structure, eligibility requirements and selection of Pathways participants, academic and instructional supports, non-instructional supports, staff training and development, funding and resources available to the program, about partnership building and stakeholder engagement within the department and the community to support students, technical assistance needs, and your views about factors that facilitate or hinder the implementation of Pathways and strategies to mitigate challenges encountered. We are also interested in your expectations regarding the program's outcomes and impact and in understanding the local policy context (e.g., articulation and credit transfer agreements) key to supporting this program. The interview will take between 60–90 minutes.

In addition, we will be doing classroom observation using a checklist to guide our data collection. We will observe 2–3 classes per site that are occurring during the time of our site visit. Your classroom was selected because it is a pre-college or college course and is in session during the month of the site visit.

We will use a classroom observation checklist to guide our data collection. Our interest is in understanding what instructional methods are being used, the variety of instructional activities that occur, whether individualized learning is occurring, the degree to which students are working in groups, what instructional supports (e.g., peer tutors) are utilized, and if technology is being utilized. This will enable us to better describe the context of Pathways and how Pathways classes are being structured across the sites.

We are not evaluating specific classes or students or instructors. No information will be collected about students or instructors. The data collection checklist will not include information about any comments instructors (or students) may make during the observation period. We will assign RAND IDs to the classrooms so that no single class or individual can be identified.

4. PAYMENT

You will not receive any remuneration for participating in these interviews.

5. RISKS OF PARTICIPATION

The names of the interviewees and their agencies will not be included in the evaluation report. This enables us to reduce the possibility of inference being used to identify potential respondents. We will ask you to respond only in your official capacity as a representative of your agency, so the risks of participation should be minimal.

6. BENEFITS OF PARTICIPATION

By participating in these interviews, you will contribute to a national evaluation of the Pathways program. The findings from this implementation study will help us understand what are the core program components and how are they being implemented across the pilot states, factors that facilitate and hindered implementation and how challenges are being addressed, what coordination activities have been undertaken, what policies or procedures were put into place at the department-level and community- or state-levels to facilitate program design and implementation, what are the support needs of the pilot programs, and what are the early lessons learned across the states.

7. CONFIDENTIALITY

We will use the information from the interviews and what we learn from the classroom observations for research purposes only. We will protect the confidentiality of this information, and will not disclose the identities of the classroom, students, or instructors, although states may be identified by name in the project's final report. We will store your answers under a code number, not your name. We will not identify you personally in any reports we write. We will destroy all information that identifies you at the end of the study. De-identified data may be kept after the study indefinitely.

All project notes, classroom checklists, and information used to identify you will be kept in locked file cabinets on office premises—electronic records will be protected by password and/or encryption—and will not be shared with anyone outside of this project. After completion of the study, all written materials will be destroyed 12 months after the report has been completed.

8. VOLUNTARY PARTICIPATION

Your participation in the study and interviews and classroom observation is completely voluntary. You may refuse to participate, refuse to answer any question in the interview, or stop participating at any time and for any reason, without any penalty. Please feel free to raise any questions or concerns at any point in time. We will be taking detailed notes, simply because we do not want to miss any of your comments. Please don't feel that you need to share information that is extremely personal or private. You are free to skip any questions that you prefer not to answer, and at any time during the discussion, should you decide to no longer participate, please indicate that you no longer wish to continue, and you will be free to leave.

9. WHOM TO CONTACT

If you have any questions or comments about this study, you are welcome to contact the evaluation project leader for this study, Lois Davis, RAND Corporation, 1776 Main Street, PO Box 2138, Santa Monica, CA 90407, tel. (310) 393-0411.

If you have questions about the Pathways demonstration project, please contact Mr. Fred Patrick, Vera Institute of Justice, 233 Broadway, New York, NY, 10279, tel. (212) 334-1300.

If you have concerns about study participation, please contact the RAND Human Subjects Protection Committee, 1776 Main Street, PO Box 2138, Santa Monica, CA 90407, tel. (310) 393-0411, ext. 6369.

Pathways from Prison to Postsecondary Education

Prisoners: Focus group discussion guide

Pathways Participants

- Inmate students participating in the Pathways post-secondary education program within the three pilot states (NJ, MI, and NC) will be invited to participate in a focus group discussion that will cover the following topics. These individuals will be current student participants in-prison classes being conducted as part of the demonstration project within each pilot state.

Focus Group Topics

- Early experiences with the Pathways program
- Motivation for applying to Pathways program
- Educational goals and how the program may help them meet those goals
- Program features (e.g., courses, academic/instructional supports, non-instructional supports, other supports)
- Perceptions about program impact on reentry, family, and non-eligible inmates
- Perceptions of the program's strengths and weaknesses
- Plans for enrolling/continuing post-secondary education upon release from prison
- Views regarding support needs
- Perceptions about program quality, usefulness, and effectiveness

Focus Group Questions

Overview of Focus Group [5 minutes]
Thank you for coming today. I want to introduce myself and the others working on this project. My name is ____ and this is ____ [Introduce focus group leader and team member]. RAND is a research organization located in California with expertise in education and public safety. We are here to learn about the Pathways program by talking to students such as yourselves who are involved in the program. We'd like to learn about your experiences—why you joined, what you think about the program activities and whether you think it's helpful for you and would be for others like you. That is the topic of our focus group today.

- Before we begin, I'd like to talk about a few ground rules. Explain who we are and the purpose of interview/focus group.
- Review oral consent form including that participation is voluntary, overview of the group process, and explanation of confidentiality guarantee. Answer any questions participants may have.
- Provide guidelines for the focus group process.
- Ask if it is okay to tape the focus group for note-taking purposes only—this

information will be kept confidential (only members of the research team will review this information).
- Ask if there are any questions before getting started.

Student Introductions [10 minutes]
To begin our discussion, I'd like to go around the room and ask each of you to introduce yourself.
- Please tell us what name you'd like to use for this discussion. It can be your own name or a name of your choosing.
- How long have you been in prison?

Education Background
Next, we would like to learn more about your education experience and goals.

- What level of education did you complete prior to being incarcerated?
  - Prompts: High school diploma? GED? Some high school?
- What education programs, if any, have you participated in since being incarcerated (other than the Pathways program)?
  - Prompts: Adult education? GED prep? Vocational programs? Postsecondary education (correspondence or prison-based)?
- What motivated you to apply for the Pathways program?
- What are your educational goals?
  - How do you think the program will help you meet those goals?

Pathways Experience
Now, we would like to learn more about your early experiences in the Pathways program.

- What courses are you taking?
  - Prompts: [Will need to add names of courses from each site.]
- What academic and instructional supports are you receiving?
  - Prompts: [Will need to add names of supports from each site.]
- What non-instructional supports are you receiving?
  - Prompts: [Will need to add names of non-instructional supports from each site.]
- What other supports do you need, but are not currently receiving?
- What are your plans for enrolling and continuing your education upon release?
  - How do you think the program will help you meet those goals?
- What do you think will be your biggest challenges when released and how might the program help you address those challenges?
- What do you think the effects of this program will be?
  - How will it affect your reentry process?
  - How will it affect your family?

   o   How might it affect other inmates who were not eligible for the program?

Wrap-up

We would like to wrap-up our discussion, by asking for your general views of the Pathways program and any advice you have for the administrators and instructors.

- In your view, what are the strongest features of the program?
  - o   What are the weakest?
- What advice would you give administrators and instructors implementing the Pathways program?
- What advice would you give to other individuals contemplating joining the Pathways program?

Closing Remarks

- Thank participant(s) for their thoughts and suggestions.
- Remind the participant(s) about how the information will be used and will be kept confidential.
- Ask participant(s) if there are any remaining questions.

RAND Corporation

EVALUATION OF THE PATHWAYS FROM PRISON TO POST-SECONDARY EDUCATION PROGRAM

FOCUS GROUP ORAL CONSENT FORM

Introduction

Thank you for coming today. I want to introduce myself and the others working on this project. My name is _____ and this is _____ [Introduce focus group leader and team member]. RAND is a research organization located in California with expertise in education and public safety. We are here to learn about the Pathways program by talking to students such as yourselves who are involved in the program. We'd like to learn about your experiences—why you joined, what you think about the program activities and whether you think it's helpful for you and would be for others like you. That is the topic of our focus group today.

Before we begin, I'd like to talk about a few ground rules.

Voluntariness

This is a research project being conducted by the RAND Corporation. Participation in this focus group is voluntary. Your release date, terms of supervision, medical care, or your general living conditions will not be affected by whether you choose to be in the study or if you choose to stop participating at any point. You may refuse to answer questions or stop taking part in the study at any time. Participation or refusal to participate in the discussion today will have no effect on your parole/post-release or on your participation in the Pathways program.

Department of Public Safety (DPS) staff are not conducting this research project. They will not get a copy of your name or of your answers. The Department may receive a copy of the overall results at the end of the study but will not be able to identify you personally from the copy they receive. You should know that if you indicate plans to harm yourself, to harm someone else, or to escape or abscond supervision that information is not confidential and will immediately be reported to Department of Public Safety staff.

Group Process

Our focus group today will last about 60–90 minutes. We are going to ask you a number of things about the program, including what interested you in the program, what your educational goals are, what courses you are taking, what you like and don't like about the program, what your support needs are, and your thoughts about ways to improve the program. We want you to answer as best as you can. We're interested in your opinions and whatever they are is fine with us. Don't worry about having a different opinion than someone else. There are no right or wrong answers. You may not agree with what others say and they may not agree with you. That is okay.

Because we have limited time, I may have to interrupt someone to move us to another topic. Please don't say anything you wouldn't want others to know and talk about. You should know, though, that if you indicate plans to harm yourself, to harm someone else, or to escape prison or abscond supervision, we are required to immediately report it to the Department of Public Safety staff.

We really appreciate your being here today with us. At the end of the focus group discussion, we will give you information about our organization and about the Pathways Demonstration Project.

Confidentiality

RAND will use the information you provide during this focus group for research purposes only. RAND will keep confidential the identities of those who participate in the focus group and will not attribute any comments to any specific individuals. We request that each of you also protect the confidentiality of others in the group. Please do not use the name or other identifying information of anyone as you talk about them, and do not repeat anything that is said here in a way that is attributable to particular people.

However, RAND cannot guarantee that everything you say during this discussion will be kept confidential by all the participants, so please do not say anything that you do not want anyone else to know.

And finally, we will be taking notes during the session because we don't want to miss any of your comments. We will assign a Study ID to each of you in the notes and will not be using your names in the written notes in order to keep confidentiality. This way we will not be able to connect the information in the written notes with your name or anything that identifies you.

If anyone prefers not to participate in the focus group discussion today, we have arranged for you to participate in an alternative activity (e.g., study hall or computer lab time). You are free to go to that activity now.

Is this okay with everyone? Are there any questions?

Questions

For questions or comments about the study, you are welcome to contact the evaluation project leader for this study, Lois Davis, RAND Corporation, 1776 Main Street, PO Box 2138, Santa Monica, CA, 90407, tel. (310) 393-0411.

If you have concerns about study participation, please contact the RAND Human Subjects Protection Committee, RAND Corporation, 1776 Main Street, PO Box 2138, Santa Monica, CA, 90407, tel. (310) 393-0411, ext. 6369.

Consent Protocols and Focus Group Discussion Guide for Evaluation of the Community Component of the North Carolina Pathways Program

RAND Corporation

EVALUATION OF THE NORTH CAROLINA PATHWAYS FROM PRISON TO POST-SECONDARY EDUCATION PROGRAM

INTERVIEW ORAL CONSENT FORM FOR PATHWAYS STUDENTS WHO WERE REINCARCERATED DURING THE STUDY PERIOD

Introduction

Thank you for taking the time to talk with us today. My name is _____ and this is _____ [Introduce the other team member or note-taker]. RAND is a private, non-profit, public policy research organization [OR I work for RTI International]. We have received a grant from the Laughing Gull Foundation and the Vera Institute of Justice to conduct an evaluation of North Carolina's Pathways Program.

Before we begin, I'd like to review with you the consent form.

For this evaluation study, we are here to learn about the Pathways Program and individuals' experiences with it by talking to individuals such as yourself. We'd like to learn about your experiences out in the community, what your educational goals were, what factors facilitated or hindered your reentry process, in what ways if any did the Pathways Program assist you, what college courses you were enrolled in and supports provided, what your current plans are, and what you think would be helpful to you and for others like you moving forward. The interview will take approximately 45–60 minutes.

Participation in this interview is voluntary. Your release date, terms of supervision, medical care, or your general living conditions will not be affected by whether you choose to be in the study or if you choose to stop participating at any point. You may refuse to answer questions or stop taking part in the study at any time. Participation or refusal to participate in the discussion today will have no effect on your parole/post-release or on your continued involvement with the Pathways program. Please feel free to raise any questions or concerns at any point in time.

This is a research project being conducted by the RAND Corporation; it is not being conducted by the North Carolina Department of Public Safety (DPS). RAND will keep confidential your comments. DPS staff will not get a copy of your answers. The Department may receive a copy of the overall results at the end of the study but will not be able to identify you personally from the copy they receive. You should know that if you indicate plans to harm yourself, to harm someone else, or to escape or abscond supervision, that information is not confidential and will immediately be reported to Department of Public Safety staff.

RAND will use the information you provide during this interview for research purposes only. The information provided will help us to understand the experiences of Pathways students with the Program and help us in evaluating the outcomes of the NC Pathways Program. The findings will be summarized in an evaluation report. In our reporting, you will be referred to only as a Pathways interviewee.

Lastly, we will be taking detailed notes, simply because we do not want to miss any of your comments.

Do I have your permission to proceed with the interview?

[IF NO:] Thank you anyway.

Potential Risks of Participation
To reduce the chance that someone might be able to find that you participated in this study, our report won't include your name or the names of the other people we are interviewing. The North Carolina Department of Public Safety (DPS) staff will not get a copy of your answers. The Department may receive a copy of the overall results at the end of the study but will not be able to identify you personally from the copy they receive.

Potential Benefits of Participation

Please note that you may not be helped directly by participating in this study. However, others may be helped by what is learned from this research. By participating in these interviews, you will contribute to a national evaluation of the Pathways program. The findings from this evaluation will help us understand how the Pathways model was implemented in North Carolina, factors that facilitated or hindered implementation within the community as well as the reentry process, what are the support needs of the Pathways students and Program staff, and what are the lessons learned in North Carolina that will be relevant to other states interested in replicating this program model.

Questions

If you have any questions or concerns about the research, please feel free to contact the study leader for this study, Lois Davis, at (310) 393-0411, ext. 7330. She is at the RAND Corporation, 1776 Main Street, Santa Monica, CA, 90407-2138.

If you have questions regarding your rights as a research subject, contact the Human Subjects Protection Committee at the RAND Corporation, 1776 Main Street, Santa Monica, CA, 90407-2138, or by phone at (866) 697-5620, or by emailing hspcinfo@rand.org.

RAND Corporation

EVALUATION OF THE NORTH CAROLINA PATHWAYS FROM PRISON TO POST-SECONDARY EDUCATION PROGRAM

Consent Protocol for State-level and Local-level Interviewees: NC Department of Public Safety and College Administrators/Pathways Program Staff/ Reentry Staff/College Staff

Project Leader: Lois Davis (PI)
Tel. 310-393-0411
Email: lmdavis@rand.org; rbozick@rand.org

1. PURPOSE OF THE STUDY

The RAND Corporation, a non-profit research institution in Santa Monica, California, is conducting an evaluation of North Carolina's (NC) Pathways from Prison to Post-Secondary Education Program. The NC Pathways Program is part of a three-state demonstration project being led by the Vera Institute of Justice. This particular evaluation is being funded by the Laughing Gull Foundation and the Vera Institute of Justice.

The NC Pathways Program has received incentive funding and technical assistance to expand access to higher education for people in prison and those recently released. The program seeks to determine whether access to postsecondary education, combined with supportive reentry services, can increase educational credentials, reduce recidivism, and increase employability and earnings. The RAND Corporation, in partnership with RTI International, was selected to conduct an independent evaluation of this program. This consent form pertains to the evaluation study being conducted by RAND and RTI International.

2. HOW WE SELECTED YOU

We are interviewing Pathways administrators, program staff, and instructors to understand the implementation of the NC Pathways Program. We selected you because of your involvement with the NC Pathways Program in one of these capacities.

3. WHAT WE WILL ASK YOU TO DO

For this evaluation study, we are interested in learning about Pathways program planning, program components, academic and instructional supports, noninstructional supports, successes and challenges, funding and resources available to the program, about partnership building and stakeholder engagement within the department and the community to support Pathways students as they transition out into the community. We are also interested in technical assistance needs, and your views about factors that facilitate or hinder the implementation of the Pathways Program and the reentry process, as well as strategies to mitigate challenges encountered. Lastly, we will be asking about your expectations regarding the program's outcomes and impact and in understanding the local policy context (e.g., articulation and credit transfer agreements) key to supporting this program. The interview will take between 60-90 minutes.

The information provided from your comments will be used by the evaluation team to evaluate the outcomes of the NC Pathways Program. The findings will be summarized in an evaluation report. To honor your privacy, your full name will not be used in any form and therefore will not be associated with any comments made. In our reporting, you will be referred to only as an administrator, instructor, or program staff interviewee. Other material used to initially identify you will be destroyed shortly after this interview.

All project notes and information used to identify you will be kept in locked file cabinets on office premises—electronic records will be protected by password and/or encryption—and will not be shared with anyone outside of this project. After completion of the study, all written materials will be destroyed 12 months after the report has been completed.

Your assistance and participation in this study is essential to the success of our research, so your time and cooperation is most appreciated.

4. PAYMENT
You will not receive any remuneration for participating in these interviews.

5. RISKS OF PARTICIPATION
To reduce the chance that someone might be able to find that you participated in this study, our report won't include your name or the names of the other people we are interviewing. We will ask you to respond only in your official capacity as a representative of your agency, so the risks of participation should be minimal.

6. BENEFITS OF PARTICIPATION
By participating in these interviews, you will contribute to a national evalu-

ation of the Pathways Program. The findings from this evaluation will help us understand what the core program components are and how the Pathways model was implemented in North Carolina, factors that facilitated or hindered implementation within the facility, within the community, as well as the reentry process. How challenges are being addressed, what coordination activities have been undertaken, what policies or procedures were put into place at the department-level and community- or state-levels to facilitate program design and implementation, what are the support needs of the Pathways students and Program staff, and what are the lessons learned in North Carolina that will be relevant to other states interested in replicating this program model.

7. CONFIDENTIALITY

We will use the information you give us for research purposes only. We will protect the confidentiality of this information and will not disclose your identity. We will store your answers under a code number, not your name. We will not identify you personally in any reports we write. We will destroy all information that identifies you at the end of the study. De-identified data may be kept after the study indefinitely.

8. VOLUNTARY PARTICIPATION

Your participation in the study and interviews is completely voluntary. You may refuse to participate, refuse to answer any question in the interview, or stop participating at any time and for any reason, without any penalty. Please feel free to raise any questions or concerns at any point in time. We will be taking detailed notes, simply because we do not want to miss any of your comments. You are free to skip any questions that you prefer not to answer, and at any time during the discussion, should you decide to no longer participate, please indicate that you no longer wish to continue, and you will be free to leave.

9. WHOM TO CONTACT

If you have any questions about this evaluation, you are welcome to contact the RAND project leader for this study, Lois Davis, RAND Corporation, tel. (310) 393-0411, ext. 7330, Email: lmdavis@rand.org.

If you have questions about the overall Pathways demonstration project, please contact Fred Patrick, Vera Institute of Justice, tel. (212) 376-3173, Email: Fpatrick@vera.org

If you have questions, comments, or concerns about the research study in general, please contact the RAND Human Subjects Protection Committee, 1776 Main Street, Santa Monica CA 90407, (866) 697-5620 or by emailing hspcinfo@ rand.org.

North Carolina Pathways from Prison to Community College

Interview and Focus Group Protocols: Informants, Topics, and Questions

<u>Interview and Focus Group Informants</u>

- Pathway students who have been released
- Local-level:
  - o Reentry staff (e.g., reentry coordinators, Pathway Navigators, job placement specialists, probation and parole supervisors)
  - o Community college administrators/coordinators
  - o Community college education staff
  - o If applicable, prison education staff, case managers, and/or counselors
- State-level:
  - o State staff responsible for implementing Pathways

<u>Interview and Focus Group Topics</u>

- **Student-level:**
  - o Update on students' experiences with Pathways in the correctional facilities
    - ▪ Motivation for applying to Pathways program
    - ▪ Educational goals and how the program has helped them to meet their goals
    - ▪ Strengths and weakness of the program features (e.g., courses, academic/instructional supports, non-instructional supports, other supports)
  - o Experiences with transition to the community
    - ▪ Pre-release planning and meetings
    - ▪ Immediate post-release supports
    - ▪ Designated release community (e.g., same or different than home community)
  - o Experiences with Pathways out in the community
    - ▪ College enrollment process
    - ▪ Course offerings
    - ▪ Academic and instructional supports (e.g., academic counseling and tutoring)
    - ▪ Non-instructional supports that complement classroom activities (e.g., Pathways Navigator, computers, transportation, childcare, housing)
    - ▪ Other reentry services
    - ▪ Views regarding program's strengths/weaknesses and additional support needed
    - ▪ For those students who did not enroll in college after release:

- Reasons for not enrolling
- Future plans to pursue their college education
- Factors important in their decision not to pursue their education
- Experiences in finding employment, family reunification
- Views regarding their reentry experience
  - o Program outcomes and impact
    - Credentials earned
    - Plans for continuing postsecondary education
    - Perceptions about program effect and impact on reentry, family/friends, transition to community-based postsecondary education, and employment opportunities
    - Perceptions about program quality, usefulness, and effectiveness
- **Program-level: (reentry and college staff)**
  - o Implementation of Pathways out in community
    - Factors facilitating implementation
    - Challenges encountered and strategies adopted to mitigate them
    - Adjustments made to original design
      - Changes in plans for pre-release and post-incarceration activities
      - Changes in state, college, or other partners' policies or procedures
      - Changes in infrastructure, facilities, and other resources supporting program
      - Changes in partners and stakeholders to support students in the community
    - Perceptions of the program's strengths and weaknesses
  - o Program components
    - Program planning (e.g., overall program design, how program fits with overall college programming or reentry services)
    - Course structure and planning (e.g., academic, vocational, and remedial)
    - Academic/instructional supports (e.g., enrollment management, academic counseling, and tutoring)
    - Non-instructional supports that complement classroom activities (e.g., computers, transportation, childcare, housing)
    - Staff training and development
    - Other program supports from college system or state DOC

- o Program outcomes and impact
  - Transition to postsecondary education in community
  - Credentials earned
  - Employment opportunities
  - Perceptions about program effect and impact on reentry and family/friends
  - Perceptions about program quality, usefulness, and effectiveness
- o Plans for sustainability
- **State-level: (Pathway coordinator)**
  - o Implementation of Pathways out in the community
    - Factors facilitating implementation
    - Challenges encountered and strategies adopted to mitigate them
    - Adjustments made to original design
      - Changes in plans for pre-release and post-incarceration activities
      - Changes in state, college, or other partners' policies or procedures
      - Changes in infrastructure, facilities, and other resources supporting program
      - Changes in partners and stakeholders to support students in the community
    - Perceptions of the program's strengths and weaknesses
    - Update on data collection
  - o Program outcomes and impact
    - Transition to postsecondary education in community
    - Credentials earned
    - Employment opportunities
    - Perceptions about program effect and impact on reentry and family/friends
    - Perceptions about program quality, usefulness, and effectiveness
  - o Plans for sustainability

References

Adams, Don, and Joel Fischer, "The Effects of Prison Residents' Community Contacts on Recidivism Rates," *Corrective and Social Psychiatry*, Vol. 22, No. 4, 1976, pp. 21–27.

Binswanger, Ingrid A., Marc F. Stern, Richard A. Deyo, Patrick J. Heagerty, Allen Cheadle, Joann G. Elmore, and Thomas D. Koepsell, "Release from Prison—A High Risk of Death for Former Inmates," *New England Journal of Medicine*, Vol. 35, 2007, pp. 157–165 [see also erratum, p. 536].

Blasko, Brandy L., Peter D. Friedmann, Anne Giuranna Rhodes, and Faye S. Taxman, "The Parolee–Parole Officer Relationship as a Mediator of Criminal Justice Outcomes," *Criminal Justice and Behavior*, Vol. 42, No. 7, 2015, pp. 722–740.

Bozick, Robert, Jennifer Steele, Lois M. Davis, and Susan Turner, "Does Providing Inmates with Education Improve Postrelease Outcomes? A Meta-Analysis of Correctional Education Programs in the United States," *Journal of Experimental Criminology*, Vol. 14, No. 3, September 2018, pp. 389–428.

Crayton, Anna, and Suzanne Rebecca Neusteter, "The Current State of Correctional Education," New York: John Jay College of Criminal Justice, Prisoner Reentry Institute, 2008.

Davis, Lois M., Robert Bozick, Jennifer L. Steele, Jessica Saunders, and Jeremy N. V. Miles, *Evaluating the Effectiveness of Correctional Education: A Meta-Analysis of Programs That Provide Education to Incarcerated Adults*, Santa Monica, Calif.: RAND Corporation, RR-266-BJA, 2013. As of April 4, 2019:
https://www.rand.org/pubs/research_reports/RR266.html

Davis, Lois M., Jennifer L. Steele, Robert Bozick, Malcolm V. Williams, Susan Turner, Jeremy N. V. Miles, Jessica Saunders, and Paul S. Steinberg, *How Effective Is Correctional Education, and Where Do We Go from Here? The Results of a Comprehensive Evaluation*, Santa Monica, Calif.: RAND Corporation, RR-564-BJA, 2014. As of April 4, 2019:
https://www.rand.org/pubs/research_reports/RR564.html

Durose, Matthew R., Alexia D. Cooper, and Howard N. Snyder, *Recidivism of Prisoners Released in 30 States in 2005: Patterns from 2005 to 2010*, Washington, D.C.: Bureau of Justice Statistics, U.S. Department of Justice, April 2014.

Erisman, Wendy, and Jeanne Bayer Contardo, *Learning to Reduce Recidivism: A 50-State Analysis of Postsecondary Correctional Education Policy*, Washington, D.C.: Institute for Higher Education Policy, November 2005.

Gorgol, Laura E., and Brian A. Sponsler, *Unlocking Potential: Results of a National Survey of Postsecondary Education in State Prisons*, Washington, D.C.: Institute for Higher Education Policy, May 2011.

Hairston, Creasie Finney, "The Importance of Families in Prisoners' Community Reentry," *ICCA Journal on Community Corrections*, April 2002.

Jonson, Cheryl Lero, and Francis T. Cullen, "Prisoner Reentry Programs," *Crime and Justice*, Vol. 44, No. 1, 2015, pp. 517–575.

Kennealy, Patrick J., Jennifer L. Skeem, Sarah M. Manchak, and Jennifer Eno Louden, "Firm, Fair, and Caring Officer-Offender Relationships Protect Against Supervision Failure," *Law and Human Behavior*, Vol. 36, No. 6, 2012, pp. 496–505.

Kreighbaum, Andrew, "Removing Barriers to Higher Ed," *Inside Higher Education*, October 11, 2018. As of April 4, 2019:
https://www.insidehighered.com/news/2018/10/11/
senator-brian-schatz-wants-college-access-students-criminal-histories

Langan, Patrick A., and David J. Levin, *Recidivism of Prisoners Released in 1994*, Washington, D.C.: Bureau of Justice Statistics, U.S. Department of Justice, June 2002.

La Vigne, Nancy G., Christy Visher, and Jennifer Castro, *Chicago Prisoners' Reflections on Returning Home*, Washington, D.C.: Urban Institute, 2004.

National Research Council, *Parole, Desistance from Crime, and Community Integration*, Washington, D.C.: National Academies Press, 2008.

NCDPS—*See* North Carolina Department of Public Safety.

North Carolina Department of Public Safety, "Craggy Correctional Center," webpage, undated(a). As of April 4, 2019:
https://www.ncdps.gov/adult-corrections/prisons/prison-facilities/craggy-correctional-center

———, "Program Services," webpage, undated(b). As of April 4, 2019:
https://www.ncdps.gov/adult-corrections/prisons/programs

———, "Proposal: Pathways from Prison to Postsecondary Education," Raleigh, 2012, unpublished document provided to RAND.

———, "Pathways from Prison to Postsecondary Education Project Standard Operating Procedure," Raleigh, January 2014, unpublished document provided to RAND.

Petersilia, Joan, *When Prisoners Come Home: Parole and Prisoner Reentry*, New York: Oxford University Press, 2003.

Travis, Jeremy, *But They All Come Back: Facing the Challenges of Prisoner Reentry*, Washington, D.C.: Urban Institute Press, 2005.

U.S. House of Representatives, 115th Cong., Formerly Incarcerated Reenter Society Transformed Safely Transitioning Every Person (FIRST STEP) Act, Washington, D.C., H.R. 5682, May 23, 2018.

U.S. Senate, 115th Cong., Restoring Education and Learning (REAL) Act of 2018, Washington, D.C., S. 2423, February 13, 2018.

Vera Institute of Justice, "Request for Proposals: Evaluation of the Pathways from Prison to Postsecondary Education Demonstration," 2012a, unpublished document provided to RAND.

———, "Unlocking Potential: Pathways from Prison to Postsecondary Education, Request for Proposals," 2012b, unpublished document provided to RAND.

———, *Pathways from Prison to Postsecondary Education Project*, New York, 2014.

Visher, Christy A., and Jeremy Travis, "Transitions from Prison to Community: Understanding Individual Pathways," *Annual Review of Sociology*, Vol. 29, August 2003, pp. 89–113.

Wexler, Ellen, "Prisoners to Get 'Second Chance Pell,'" *Inside Higher Education*, June 24, 2016. As of April 4, 2019:
https://www.insidehighered.com/news/2016/06/24/us-expands-pell-grant-program-12000-prison